All About Grand Canyon: A Kid's Guide to Nature's Greatest Wonder

Educational Books For Kids, Volume 19

Shah Rukh

Published by Shah Rukh, 2024.

While every precaution has been taken in the preparation of this book, the publisher assumes no responsibility for errors or omissions, or for damages resulting from the use of the information contained herein.

ALL ABOUT GRAND CANYON: A KID'S GUIDE TO NATURE'S GREATEST WONDER

First edition. September 27, 2024.

Copyright © 2024 Shah Rukh.

ISBN: 979-8227447500

Written by Shah Rukh.

Table of Contents

Prologue

Welcome to *All About Grand Canyon: A Kid's Guide to Nature's Greatest Wonder*! Have you ever wondered what it would be like to stand on the edge of one of the world's most awe-inspiring natural creations? The Grand Canyon is a place of endless discovery, where towering cliffs, colorful rocks, and a powerful river all come together to tell the story of our planet's ancient history.

In this book, you'll embark on an adventure through time, learning how the Grand Canyon was formed over millions of years, how the mighty Colorado River continues to shape it, and how early people lived in and around its towering walls. From exploring hidden caves to meeting the animals that call the canyon home, each chapter will take you deeper into this incredible natural wonder.

But the Grand Canyon isn't just about looking into the past. It's also a place of adventure today! You'll find out what it's like to hike its famous trails, raft along the rushing river, and even walk on the Skywalk, a glass bridge that lets you look down into the canyon's depths.

Whether you dream of visiting the Grand Canyon one day or just want to learn all about this fascinating place, you're in for an exciting journey. So, grab your backpack, put on your explorer hat, and get ready to discover the wonders of the Grand Canyon!

Chapter 1: The Formation of the Grand Canyon

The formation of the Grand Canyon is one of the most fascinating and complex geological processes in Earth's history, spanning millions of years. Located in northern Arizona, the Grand Canyon stands as one of the planet's most iconic natural wonders, with its vast expanse and multicolored rock layers revealing an incredible timeline of Earth's geological past. The story of how this massive canyon came to be is deeply tied to the movements of the Earth's crust, the forces of erosion, and the relentless work of water, wind, and time.

To understand how the Grand Canyon formed, we have to travel back in time, hundreds of millions of years, to an era when this region looked completely different. The land that we now recognize as the Grand Canyon was once submerged under ancient seas. Over time, these seas deposited layers of sediment that would eventually harden into rock. These sedimentary rocks, which make up the striking layers of the Grand Canyon, are composed of limestone, sandstone, and shale. These rocks tell a story of a landscape that has transformed dramatically over eons, from shallow oceans to deserts, and everything in between.

Around 1.8 billion years ago, the oldest rocks in the Grand Canyon, known as the Vishnu Schist, began to form. These rocks were created through intense heat and pressure deep within the Earth's crust, during a period of tectonic activity. Volcanic eruptions, earthquakes, and the collision of continental plates caused these rocks to fold, break, and metamorphose into their current form. Over time, these ancient rocks were uplifted and eventually became the foundation upon which the rest of the Grand Canyon's layers were built. The Vishnu Schist is visible today at the base of the canyon, offering a glimpse into Earth's deep past.

However, the Grand Canyon as we recognize it today did not begin to take shape until much more recently, geologically speaking. About 70 million years ago, during a period known as the Laramide Orogeny, the region underwent a dramatic transformation. The Laramide Orogeny was a period of mountain building caused by the subduction of oceanic plates beneath the North American Plate. This process uplifted large sections of the Earth's crust, creating the Rocky Mountains and the Colorado Plateau, where the Grand Canyon is located. This uplift was critical in the formation of the canyon, as it raised the land high above sea level, allowing rivers to begin carving into the rock.

As the Colorado Plateau rose, so too did the ancient layers of sediment that had been deposited over millions of years. These rock layers, now exposed to the forces of erosion, became vulnerable to the elements. The most important factor in the Grand Canyon's formation was the Colorado River, which began its work around 5 to 6 million years ago. Over millions of years, this powerful river slowly carved its way through the uplifted plateau, slicing through the various layers of rock and creating the canyon we see today. The river's ability to cut through solid rock was due in part to the uplift of the plateau, which increased the river's speed and erosive power.

But the Colorado River didn't act alone. The process of erosion was aided by other forces as well. Wind, rain, and the freeze-thaw cycle played crucial roles in shaping the canyon. During the day, temperatures would rise, causing water from rain or snowmelt to seep into cracks in the rock. At night, when temperatures dropped, the water would freeze and expand, causing the rock to crack and break apart. Over time, this freeze-thaw cycle widened the canyon and deepened its walls, helping to sculpt the jagged cliffs and steep slopes that define the Grand Canyon today.

Another important aspect of the Grand Canyon's formation is the role of geological faults. As the Colorado Plateau was uplifted, it also experienced faulting, where the Earth's crust cracked and shifted. These faults created fractures in the rock, which allowed the river and other erosive forces to exploit weaknesses in the Earth's crust, carving out deeper and more dramatic sections of the canyon. One prominent fault in the region is the Bright Angel Fault, which runs through the Grand Canyon and has influenced its shape and orientation.

The different layers of rock within the Grand Canyon tell a story of changing environments and ancient ecosystems. For example, the red rock layers, known as the Supai Group, were formed during a time when the region was a vast, arid desert. Other layers, like the bright white limestone of the Kaibab Formation, were deposited when the area was covered by a shallow sea teeming with marine life. These layers provide valuable clues to scientists about the Earth's history and the many changes that have occurred over millions of years. Fossils of ancient marine creatures, plants, and even early reptiles have been found within the canyon's walls, adding to the rich tapestry of its geological history.

The Grand Canyon's formation was not a single, linear process but rather a combination of various events and forces acting over different periods of time. Volcanic activity has also played a role in shaping the canyon. Around one million years ago, volcanic eruptions in the region spewed lava into the canyon, temporarily damming the Colorado River and creating small lakes. Eventually, these lava dams were breached, and the river continued its course, but the volcanic rock remains visible in some parts of the canyon.

Today, the Grand Canyon continues to evolve. Erosion is an ongoing process, with the Colorado River still cutting into the rock, though at a much slower rate than in the past. The canyon also experiences landslides, rockfalls, and other natural events that gradually change its shape. Scientists estimate that the Grand Canyon will continue to deepen and widen over the coming millions of years, as the forces of nature persist in their work.

In addition to its geological significance, the Grand Canyon has also played an important role in the history of human civilization. For thousands of years, Native American tribes have lived in and around the canyon, drawing on its resources and finding spiritual significance in its awe-inspiring landscapes. The canyon's formation is not just a story of rocks and rivers, but also of the deep connection between people and the natural world.

In conclusion, the formation of the Grand Canyon is a story that spans billions of years, involving ancient seas, tectonic forces, volcanic eruptions, and the relentless work of erosion. From the uplift of the Colorado Plateau to the carving power of the Colorado River, the Grand Canyon stands as a testament to the incredible forces that have shaped our planet. Each layer of rock within the canyon tells a story of a different time in Earth's history, and the canyon itself continues to evolve as nature's forces persist. Today, the Grand Canyon remains one of the most breathtaking and iconic landscapes on Earth, offering a window into the deep past and a reminder of the powerful geological processes that continue to shape our world.

Chapter 2: The Mighty Colorado River's Journey

The mighty Colorado River, one of the most remarkable and important rivers in North America, is the lifeblood of the Grand Canyon and has played a pivotal role in shaping not only the landscape of the American Southwest but also the lives of the people, plants, and animals that depend on its waters. Spanning over 1,450 miles, the Colorado River begins its journey in the high Rocky Mountains of Colorado and winds its way through seven U.S. states and two Mexican states before finally emptying into the Gulf of California. Its course is a testament to the extraordinary forces of nature, carving out the iconic Grand Canyon and providing water to millions of people across a vast desert region.

The Colorado River's journey begins high in the snow-capped peaks of the Rocky Mountains, where snowmelt and rainfall feed its headwaters. This pristine water flows through the forests and meadows of Colorado, gradually picking up speed as it descends into the arid regions of the American Southwest. The river's upper stretches are relatively narrow and fast-moving, cutting through the steep valleys and canyons of the Rockies. Along the way, it is joined by numerous tributaries, which help to increase its volume and power. These early stages of the river's journey are crucial, as they supply water not only to the river itself but also to the ecosystems and communities that rely on this precious resource.

As the Colorado River flows out of the Rockies and into the high desert of the Colorado Plateau, its character begins to change. The river widens, and its pace slows as it encounters the vast open spaces of the Southwest. This is where the river begins its most famous work: the carving of the Grand Canyon. Over millions of years, the Colorado River has tirelessly cut through the rock layers of the Colorado Plateau, creating one of the most awe-inspiring natural wonders on Earth. The sheer power of the river's erosive forces is on full display in the Grand Canyon, where it has sliced through nearly two billion years of Earth's geological history, exposing ancient rock formations and creating the steep cliffs and deep chasms that define the canyon today.

The carving of the Grand Canyon is a testament to the incredible power of water and time. The Colorado River's ability to erode rock is due in large part to the steep gradient of the Colorado Plateau, which causes the river to flow with tremendous speed and force. As the river cuts through the various layers of sedimentary rock, it carries away millions of tons of material, gradually deepening and widening the canyon over millions of years. This process continues today, although at a much slower rate than in the past, as the river continues to shape the landscape of the Grand Canyon.

The Colorado River's journey through the Grand Canyon is perhaps its most dramatic and iconic phase, but the river's influence extends far beyond the canyon's walls. Downstream of the Grand Canyon, the Colorado River enters an even more arid and inhospitable region: the Sonoran and Mojave Deserts. Here, the river becomes a vital source of life in an otherwise barren landscape. The river's waters support a wide variety of plant and animal species, many of which are specially adapted to survive in the harsh desert environment. Cottonwood trees, willows, and mesquite grow along the river's banks, creating a ribbon of green that stands in stark contrast to the surrounding desert. These riparian ecosystems are home to a diverse array of wildlife, including beavers, otters, birds, fish, and reptiles.

As the Colorado River continues its journey, it becomes increasingly important to human communities. The river is a critical source of water for millions of people in the American Southwest, including major cities like Las Vegas, Phoenix, Tucson, and Los Angeles. The river's water is also used to irrigate vast agricultural regions, particularly in California's Imperial Valley, which is one of the most productive farming areas in the world. The Colorado River supplies water to approximately 40 million people and irrigates over 5 million acres of farmland, making it one of the most heavily managed and controlled rivers in the world.

The management of the Colorado River is a complex and controversial issue, as the demand for its water far exceeds the river's natural flow. Over the past century, numerous dams and reservoirs have been built along the river to control its flow and distribute its water to various regions. The most famous of these is the Hoover Dam, which was completed in 1935 and created Lake Mead, the largest reservoir in the United States. The Hoover Dam not only provides water for agriculture and cities but also generates hydroelectric power, which supplies electricity to millions of people in the Southwest. Other major dams on the Colorado River include Glen Canyon Dam, which created Lake Powell, and Parker Dam, which formed Lake Havasu. These dams have transformed the river into a highly regulated system, with water allocations governed by complex agreements between the various states and Mexico.

While these dams and reservoirs have brought numerous benefits, such as providing a reliable source of water and electricity, they have also had significant environmental consequences. The construction of the dams has altered the natural flow of the Colorado River, disrupting ecosystems and impacting the species that rely on the river's natural cycles. For example, the once-mighty spring floods that would periodically sweep through the Grand Canyon, replenishing sandbars and providing critical habitat for fish and wildlife, have been largely eliminated by the dams. This has led to the decline of native species such as the humpback chub and the razorback sucker, both of which are now endangered.

In addition to the ecological impacts, the over-allocation of the Colorado River's water has created a situation where the river often no longer reaches its natural endpoint, the Gulf of California. Historically, the Colorado River flowed into the Gulf, creating a rich delta ecosystem that supported a wide variety of plant and animal species, as well as indigenous communities that relied on the river's water for fishing and farming. However, due to the extensive diversion of the river's water for agriculture and urban use, the Colorado River has not regularly reached the sea since the 1960s. The drying up of the Colorado River delta has had devastating ecological and social consequences, leading to the loss of wetlands, wildlife, and traditional livelihoods.

Despite these challenges, efforts are being made to restore the Colorado River and its ecosystems. In recent years, environmental groups, governments, and indigenous communities have come together to work on solutions to balance the needs of people with the health of the river. One notable success occurred in 2014, when an agreement was reached between the United States and Mexico to release a controlled pulse of water into the Colorado River delta, temporarily restoring flow to the dry riverbed and bringing life back to the delta for the first time in decades. This event, known as the "pulse flow," was a symbolic and hopeful moment in the ongoing efforts to restore the Colorado River's natural functions.

The Colorado River's journey is one of both natural wonder and human intervention. It has carved some of the most spectacular landscapes on Earth, including the Grand Canyon, while also providing water, power, and sustenance to millions of people. However, the river's future is uncertain, as climate change, population growth, and increasing demand for water place unprecedented strain on this vital resource. The Colorado River is already considered one of the most endangered rivers in the world, and its flow has been steadily declining in recent decades due to reduced snowpack in the Rockies, rising temperatures, and increased evaporation. As the American Southwest faces the growing threat of drought and water shortages, the challenge of managing the Colorado River's limited resources becomes ever more pressing.

In conclusion, the mighty Colorado River's journey is a tale of immense natural beauty, incredible geological processes, and the delicate balance between human needs and environmental preservation. From its origins in the snowy peaks of the Rockies to its final destination in the arid deserts of the Southwest, the Colorado River has shaped the land and sustained life for millions of years. Its role in carving the Grand Canyon is just one part of its long and complex story, a story that continues to evolve as we grapple with the challenges of conserving this vital river for future generations. The Colorado River remains a symbol of the dynamic and ever-changing relationship between nature and humanity, reminding us of both the power and fragility of the natural world.

Chapter 3: Exploring the Grand Canyon's Layers of Rock

Exploring the Grand Canyon's layers of rock is like taking a journey through time, as each layer tells a unique story about Earth's geological history, spanning nearly two billion years. The Grand Canyon, one of the most visually striking and scientifically significant landscapes on Earth, offers an unparalleled glimpse into the processes that have shaped our planet over eons. From the ancient basement rocks at the bottom of the canyon to the more recent layers near the rim, these strata provide vital clues about how environments, climates, and life on Earth have changed over time.

The Grand Canyon is approximately 277 miles long, up to 18 miles wide, and over a mile deep in places. Its vast size and the immense depth of its rock layers reveal the dramatic effects of tectonic forces, erosion, volcanic activity, and even oceanic changes that have occurred throughout Earth's history. What makes the Grand Canyon particularly unique is how clearly the different layers of rock are exposed, allowing geologists and visitors alike to study the distinct bands of rock that stack upon each other like pages in a geological book.

At the very bottom of the canyon, near the Colorado River, lies the oldest layer: the Vishnu Basement Rocks. These rocks date back nearly two billion years to a time known as the Precambrian era. The Vishnu Schist, a type of metamorphic rock, and the Zoroaster Granite make up much of the lower canyon. The intense heat and pressure from deep within the Earth transformed these rocks from their original forms into the dark, contorted bands of schist and the lighter, speckled granite. These basement rocks represent the ancient core of North America and provide a glimpse into the planet's earliest geological processes, long before life as we know it emerged.

Overlying the Vishnu Basement Rocks are the Grand Canyon Supergroup rocks, which date to around 1.2 billion to 800 million years ago. These rocks consist of a variety of sedimentary formations, including shale, sandstone, and limestone. The Supergroup layers formed when the region was part of a shallow, tropical sea. During this period, the area that is now the Grand Canyon experienced significant tectonic activity, including faulting and tilting, which caused some of the rock layers to be displaced and angled at different orientations. This tectonic activity is evident in the Great Unconformity, a striking boundary where there is a dramatic gap in the geological record, representing about 250 million years of missing rock layers. This unconformity is one of the most famous features of the Grand Canyon's stratigraphy, symbolizing a long period of erosion and non-deposition.

Moving up through the canyon's layers, we encounter the Tonto Group, which consists of three distinct formations: the Tapeats Sandstone, Bright Angel Shale, and Muav Limestone. These layers were deposited during the Cambrian period, around 525 to 505 million years ago, when the area was submerged beneath a shallow sea. The Tapeats Sandstone is a thick, coarse-grained rock that formed from the sands of ancient beaches and river deltas. Overlying the Tapeats is the Bright Angel Shale, a soft, greenish-gray rock composed of mud and clay. This layer represents a quieter, deeper marine environment where finer sediments settled out of the water. Finally, the Muav Limestone is a hard, gray rock that formed from the accumulation of calcium carbonate in a warm, shallow sea. Together, these layers tell the story of the gradual encroachment of an ancient ocean across the North American continent.

Above the Tonto Group, the canyon's middle layers consist of the Temple Butte Formation, the Redwall Limestone, and the Supai Group, which span the Devonian, Mississippian, and Pennsylvanian periods (roughly 360 to 290 million years ago). The Temple Butte

Formation is relatively thin and consists of dolomitic limestone, which formed in shallow coastal environments during the Devonian period. This layer is notable for containing fossils of marine organisms such as brachiopods and crinoids, providing evidence of the diverse life that once thrived in the seas of this time.

The Redwall Limestone, one of the most prominent and visually striking layers of the Grand Canyon, is a thick, cliff-forming unit that stretches for hundreds of miles across the region. It was deposited during the Mississippian period, when warm, shallow seas once again covered the area. The Redwall is composed mostly of limestone, but its characteristic red color comes from iron oxide staining from the layers above it. This layer is rich in fossils, including brachiopods, corals, and bryozoans, which give us insight into the marine life that flourished during the Mississippian. The sheer cliffs of the Redwall Limestone are a defining feature of the canyon's landscape, providing a dramatic contrast to the softer, more eroded layers above and below.

Above the Redwall Limestone is the Supai Group, a sequence of sandstone, siltstone, and shale layers deposited during the Pennsylvanian period. These rocks reflect a time when the area alternated between coastal marine environments and more terrestrial conditions, with periodic advances and retreats of shallow seas. The Supai Group is characterized by reddish-brown rocks, which give the canyon its distinctive color in many places. These rocks formed from the sands, silts, and clays deposited in river channels, floodplains, and coastal environments. Fossils of amphibians, reptiles, and plant material found in the Supai Group provide evidence of the transition from a predominantly marine environment to one that supported a greater diversity of terrestrial life.

Continuing upward, we encounter the Hermit Shale, Coconino Sandstone, and Toroweap Formation, which were deposited during the Permian period (around 300 to 250 million years ago). The Hermit Shale, a soft, red, and easily eroded layer, represents sediments deposited in low-lying river floodplains and coastal swamps. Fossils of ferns and other plants are found in this layer, indicating that lush vegetation once thrived here.

The Coconino Sandstone, one of the most recognizable and photogenic layers of the Grand Canyon, is a thick, white to pale-yellow rock that forms the massive cliffs seen in many parts of the canyon. This layer was deposited in a desert environment, where large sand dunes once dominated the landscape. The cross-bedded layers of the Coconino Sandstone are evidence of wind-blown dunes, similar to those found in modern desert environments. The Coconino Sandstone's stark color and cliff-forming properties make it one of the most visually striking layers in the canyon, contrasting sharply with the reddish hues of the surrounding rocks.

Above the Coconino Sandstone is the Toroweap Formation, a thinner layer of limestone and dolomite that was deposited in a shallow, evaporating sea. This layer contains evidence of periodic marine transgressions, as well as the formation of evaporite minerals such as gypsum. The presence of these minerals suggests that the area experienced a dry, arid climate during this time.

At the very top of the Grand Canyon's stratigraphic sequence is the Kaibab Limestone, the youngest of the major rock layers, which was deposited around 270 million years ago during the late Permian period. The Kaibab Limestone represents the final advance of a shallow sea across the region before the area was uplifted and the seas retreated. This layer is composed of gray, fossil-rich limestone and dolomite, and it forms the broad, flat plateau that surrounds the Grand Canyon today. Fossils of marine organisms, such as sponges, brachiopods, and crinoids, are abundant in the Kaibab Limestone, providing evidence of the diverse life that once thrived in these ancient seas.

The rock layers of the Grand Canyon are not only remarkable for their beauty and grandeur but also for the stories they tell about Earth's past. Each layer represents a different environment, from ancient seas and deserts to rivers and swamps, and each provides a unique snapshot of the conditions that existed millions of years ago. These rocks record the slow, relentless processes of erosion, deposition, and tectonic uplift that have shaped the landscape of the American Southwest over hundreds of millions of years.

The Grand Canyon's rock layers also offer insight into the life forms that once inhabited these ancient environments. Fossils found in the canyon range from simple marine organisms, such as trilobites and brachiopods, to more complex land animals, such as amphibians and reptiles. These fossils provide a window into the evolution of life on Earth, showing how species adapted to changing climates and environments over time.

Exploring the Grand Canyon's layers of rock is not just a geological journey; it is a journey through the history of our planet. From the ancient metamorphic rocks at the bottom of the canyon to the younger sedimentary layers near the top, the Grand Canyon reveals the incredible forces that have shaped the Earth and the life that has evolved in response to these changes. Each layer is a chapter in the story of our planet, and together they form one of the most complete and awe-inspiring geological records on Earth.

Chapter 4: Ancient Civilizations and the Grand Canyon

The Grand Canyon, renowned for its breathtaking geological formations, is not only a marvel of nature but also a region steeped in the fascinating history of ancient civilizations. Long before it became a renowned tourist destination, the Grand Canyon was home to several Native American cultures, each of which left their mark on the landscape, shaped by their beliefs, lifestyle, and survival strategies. These early inhabitants saw the Grand Canyon as more than just a spectacular natural wonder; they viewed it as a spiritual, cultural, and ecological sanctuary that provided sustenance and shaped their identities. The canyon and its surroundings have served as a cradle of human civilization for thousands of years, and its deep cultural significance continues to resonate today.

The history of human presence in the Grand Canyon region stretches back at least 12,000 years, to a time when nomadic hunter-gatherers roamed the North American continent at the end of the last Ice Age. These early people, known as the Paleo-Indians, were highly skilled in adapting to the often harsh and changing environments they encountered. Archaeological evidence suggests that they hunted large mammals such as mammoths and bison using stone tools, and they likely passed through the Grand Canyon region in search of game, water, and shelter. Although the Paleo-Indians left behind few permanent structures, their presence is etched into the landscape in the form of scattered artifacts, such as spear points and scrapers, which provide clues to their way of life.

As the climate began to warm and the Ice Age came to an end, the landscape of the American Southwest transformed, giving rise to new ecosystems and changing the patterns of human habitation. By around 6,000 years ago, the Archaic period had begun, and the people of the

Grand Canyon region had developed more sophisticated methods of hunting and gathering. These early inhabitants relied on a wide variety of food sources, including small game, seeds, nuts, and roots. Over time, they became increasingly skilled in managing their environment, using fire to promote the growth of edible plants and crafting tools such as atlatls (spear-throwers) to hunt with greater precision. Evidence of their presence can be found in rock shelters and caves throughout the Grand Canyon, where they left behind tools, food remnants, and other traces of their daily lives.

One of the most significant developments in the human history of the Grand Canyon region occurred around 4,000 years ago, when early agricultural practices began to take root. People in the region started to cultivate crops such as corn, beans, and squash, marking the transition from a strictly nomadic lifestyle to a more settled, agrarian way of life. This agricultural revolution allowed for the establishment of more permanent settlements, and it laid the foundation for the rise of complex societies in the Southwest. The ancient peoples who inhabited the Grand Canyon were part of a broader cultural network that included the Hohokam, Mogollon, and Ancestral Puebloans (also known as the Anasazi), three of the most influential prehistoric cultures in the American Southwest.

The Ancestral Puebloans, in particular, left a profound legacy in the Grand Canyon region. Their civilization, which flourished between approximately 500 CE and 1300 CE, was marked by remarkable advancements in architecture, agriculture, and pottery. The Ancestral Puebloans are perhaps best known for their intricate cliff dwellings, which were built into the walls of canyons and mesas to provide protection from the elements and potential enemies. Although the most famous of these dwellings are found in places like Mesa Verde in Colorado, similar structures have been discovered in the Grand Canyon, particularly in the canyon's western region.

The Ancestral Puebloans constructed sophisticated irrigation systems to manage the scarce water resources of the arid Southwest, allowing them to grow crops in challenging environments. They cultivated corn, beans, and squash in terraced gardens, and they used complex techniques such as check dams and reservoirs to capture and store rainwater. This agricultural ingenuity enabled the Ancestral Puebloans to thrive in the canyon for centuries, even in the face of frequent droughts and other environmental challenges. Their deep understanding of the land and their ability to live sustainably in harmony with their surroundings are testaments to their resilience and adaptability.

One of the most important archaeological sites in the Grand Canyon associated with the Ancestral Puebloans is known as Tusayan Ruin. Located on the South Rim of the canyon, Tusayan Ruin was once home to a small community of Puebloans who lived in stone dwellings and relied on farming to sustain themselves. The site contains the remains of a kiva, a ceremonial room used for religious and social gatherings, as well as other structures that suggest the inhabitants practiced communal living. Excavations at Tusayan Ruin have uncovered pottery, stone tools, and other artifacts that provide valuable insights into the daily lives and spiritual practices of the Puebloans who called the Grand Canyon home.

The Grand Canyon also holds significant spiritual and cultural meaning for the Havasupai and Hopi tribes, whose ancestors have lived in the region for centuries and who continue to maintain deep connections to the land. The Havasupai, known as the "People of the Blue-Green Water," have traditionally lived in a remote area of the Grand Canyon known as Havasu Canyon, where the turquoise waters of Havasu Creek flow through lush, terraced gardens and feed into breathtaking waterfalls. For the Havasupai, the Grand Canyon is not only a place of great beauty but also a sacred landscape imbued with spiritual significance. The tribe's oral traditions speak of their ancestors' long-standing relationship with the canyon, and many of their ceremonies and rituals are tied to the natural cycles of the land.

The Hopi people, whose ancestors were part of the Ancestral Puebloan culture, also consider the Grand Canyon to be a place of deep spiritual importance. According to Hopi tradition, the Grand Canyon is the site of the Sipapu, the place where their ancestors emerged from the underworld into the present world. The Hopi view the canyon as a sacred space where the boundaries between the physical and spiritual worlds are thin, and they believe that the canyon's towering cliffs and deep chasms are home to powerful spirits. Even today, the Hopi continue to visit the Grand Canyon for religious ceremonies and pilgrimages, reaffirming their ancient connections to the land.

The influence of ancient civilizations in the Grand Canyon region can also be seen in the region's rock art, which provides a unique window into the beliefs, stories, and daily lives of its early inhabitants. The walls of the canyon and its surrounding cliffs are adorned with petroglyphs and pictographs, carved or painted by the ancestors of the region's Native American tribes. These images depict a wide variety of subjects, from hunting scenes and animals to abstract symbols and representations of spiritual beings. Some of the rock art is believed to be thousands of years old, dating back to the Archaic period, while other examples are more recent, created by the Puebloans and other cultures that followed.

The meaning of much of the rock art remains a mystery, but many researchers believe that it served both practical and ceremonial purposes. Some petroglyphs may have been used to mark hunting grounds or important water sources, while others may have played a role in religious rituals or storytelling. For the descendants of the canyon's ancient inhabitants, the rock art represents a tangible connection to their ancestors, a visual record of their deep-rooted relationship with the land.

By around 1300 CE, many of the large settlements in the Grand Canyon region were abandoned. Historians and archaeologists continue to debate the reasons for this sudden decline, but it is likely that a combination of factors, including prolonged drought, resource depletion, and social conflict, contributed to the depopulation of the area. However, the descendants of the people who once lived in the Grand Canyon did not disappear. Instead, they migrated to other parts of the Southwest, where they established new communities and continued to carry on the traditions of their ancestors.

Despite the passage of centuries, the legacy of these ancient civilizations continues to shape the cultural landscape of the Grand Canyon. The Havasupai, Hopi, Navajo, Zuni, and other Native American tribes that live in the region today are the descendants of the people who first made the Grand Canyon their home. They continue to maintain strong ties to the land, preserving their traditions, languages, and spiritual beliefs while also adapting to the challenges of modern life.

The Grand Canyon's ancient civilizations left behind more than just physical artifacts; they left a legacy of resilience, adaptability, and a deep respect for the natural world. Their ability to thrive in one of the most challenging environments on Earth is a testament to their ingenuity and perseverance. Their spiritual connection to the land, expressed through their rituals, oral traditions, and artistic expressions, continues to inspire awe and reverence for this majestic landscape.

In exploring the history of the ancient civilizations that called the Grand Canyon home, we gain a deeper understanding of the canyon as not only a geological wonder but also a cultural and spiritual sanctuary. The Grand Canyon has been a place of refuge, survival, and spiritual reflection for thousands of years, and it remains a vital part of the heritage and identity of the Native American tribes who continue to honor its sacred significance today. Through their stories, traditions, and enduring presence, the ancient peoples of the Grand Canyon have left an indelible mark on this awe-inspiring landscape, reminding us that the canyon is not only a natural wonder but also a living cultural treasure.

21

Chapter 5: The Wildlife of the Grand Canyon

The Grand Canyon, a vast and awe-inspiring natural wonder, is not just a geological marvel but also a rich, diverse ecosystem teeming with wildlife. Spanning over 277 miles of the Colorado River and encompassing a range of environments from desert scrub to lush forested plateaus, the Grand Canyon is home to an astonishing variety of species that have adapted to survive in its rugged and often extreme conditions. The wildlife of the Grand Canyon includes mammals, birds, reptiles, amphibians, fish, and countless invertebrates, all of which have evolved to thrive in this unique and dynamic environment. From the arid, sunbaked lower elevations to the cooler, more temperate forests at higher altitudes, the animals of the Grand Canyon tell a fascinating story of survival, adaptation, and ecological balance.

At first glance, the Grand Canyon may seem like a harsh and unforgiving environment, particularly in its lower reaches where temperatures can soar above 100 degrees Fahrenheit in the summer, and the landscape is dominated by rocky cliffs, barren plateaus, and sparse vegetation. Yet, even in these seemingly inhospitable areas, life finds a way to flourish. One of the most iconic mammals of the canyon's arid zones is the bighorn sheep. These majestic animals, with their impressive curved horns, are perfectly adapted to life in the steep, rocky terrain. Bighorn sheep are incredible climbers, using their sure-footedness to navigate the narrow ledges and sheer cliffs of the canyon in search of food and water. Their diet consists mainly of grasses, shrubs, and other vegetation, and they have adapted to survive on very little water, a crucial skill in the canyon's desert climate. Bighorn sheep are also known for their social behavior, often living in small herds and using their agility and strength to escape predators like mountain lions.

Mountain lions, or cougars, are the top predators of the Grand Canyon, and though they are elusive and rarely seen by visitors, they play a vital role in maintaining the balance of the ecosystem. These solitary and stealthy hunters prey on a variety of animals, including deer, bighorn sheep, and smaller mammals like rabbits and squirrels. The mountain lion's territory can span hundreds of square miles, and they are highly adaptable, capable of living in a range of environments from the arid canyon floor to the cooler forested rims. Their presence helps control the populations of herbivores, preventing overgrazing and ensuring that plant life remains healthy and diverse.

In addition to the bighorn sheep and mountain lions, the Grand Canyon is home to a number of other mammal species, each uniquely suited to their environment. Mule deer, for example, are commonly seen in the canyon, particularly in the more vegetated areas near the North and South Rims. These graceful herbivores feed on grasses, shrubs, and trees, and are often spotted by hikers and visitors as they graze near the canyon's edges. Coyotes, another highly adaptable species, are also common in the canyon. These opportunistic carnivores and scavengers feed on a wide variety of food, from small mammals like rabbits and rodents to insects, fruits, and carrion. Their adaptability has allowed them to thrive in many different habitats within the canyon, from the desert lowlands to the forested plateaus.

The Grand Canyon is also home to several species of smaller mammals, including rock squirrels, ringtails, and desert cottontails. Rock squirrels are one of the most commonly encountered animals in the canyon, particularly around the visitor areas where they have become accustomed to humans. These curious rodents are highly adaptable and can be found throughout the canyon, often foraging for food near campsites and picnic areas. Ringtails, on the other hand, are more elusive and nocturnal, making them harder to spot. These small, cat-like mammals are closely related to raccoons and are known for their long, bushy tails and excellent climbing abilities. They feed on a variety of food, including insects, small mammals, fruits, and even scorpions.

Speaking of scorpions, the Grand Canyon is home to a diverse array of invertebrates, including several species of scorpions, spiders, and insects. One of the most intriguing invertebrates found in the canyon is the giant desert hairy scorpion, the largest scorpion species in North America. Despite its fearsome appearance, the sting of this scorpion is relatively harmless to humans, though it can be quite painful. These nocturnal predators feed on insects, spiders, and even small lizards, using their powerful pincers and venomous stingers to subdue their prey.

Reptiles are also a prominent part of the Grand Canyon's wildlife. With its hot, dry climate and abundance of rocky crevices and sun-soaked slopes, the canyon provides an ideal habitat for a variety of lizard and snake species. The collared lizard, with its distinctive black bands around its neck, is one of the most commonly seen reptiles in the canyon. These colorful lizards are fast and agile, capable of running on their hind legs to escape predators. They feed primarily on insects but will also eat smaller lizards and other prey. Another common lizard species is the desert spiny lizard, which is often seen basking on rocks in the sunlight. These lizards, like many other reptiles in the canyon, rely on the sun's warmth to regulate their body temperature.

The Grand Canyon is also home to several snake species, including the western diamondback rattlesnake, the most well-known venomous snake in the region. Rattlesnakes are commonly found in the canyon's lower elevations, where they hunt for rodents, birds, and other small animals. Despite their fearsome reputation, rattlesnakes are generally shy and will avoid humans if given the chance. They use their distinctive rattles as a warning to potential threats, and their camouflage allows them to blend in with the rocky terrain. Other snake species in the canyon include the gopher snake, which is non-venomous and often mistaken for a rattlesnake due to its similar coloration and patterning, and the garter snake, which can be found near the canyon's water sources.

The Grand Canyon's waterways, particularly the Colorado River, are home to a variety of fish species, many of which are endemic, meaning they are found nowhere else in the world. The humpback chub, for example, is a rare and endangered fish that has adapted to the cold, fast-flowing waters of the Colorado River. Its distinctive humpback and streamlined body allow it to navigate the river's strong currents, and it feeds on insects and small invertebrates. Another notable fish species is the razorback sucker, which is also endangered and has been the focus of extensive conservation efforts in recent years. These fish, along with others like the speckled dace and flannelmouth sucker, play a critical role in the river's ecosystem, providing food for birds, mammals, and other predators.

Birdlife in the Grand Canyon is incredibly diverse, with more than 400 species recorded in the region. The canyon's wide range of habitats, from riparian zones along the river to the forests of the North Rim, supports a variety of bird species, including some that are rare or endangered. One of the most iconic birds of the Grand Canyon is the California condor, one of the largest flying birds in the world with a wingspan of up to 9 feet. These magnificent scavengers, which were once on the brink of extinction, have been successfully reintroduced to the Grand Canyon and can occasionally be seen soaring above the canyon's cliffs in search of carrion. Their reintroduction has been one of the most remarkable conservation success stories in the region, highlighting the importance of protecting the Grand Canyon's wildlife for future generations.

Other bird species commonly seen in the Grand Canyon include the peregrine falcon, known for its incredible speed and hunting prowess, and the bald eagle, a symbol of American wildlife and a majestic sight as it soars above the canyon's vast expanse. Songbirds such as the canyon wren, with its distinctive descending call, and the western bluebird, with its vibrant blue and orange plumage, add to the rich tapestry of birdlife that can be observed in the canyon. Additionally, waterfowl such as the mallard and great blue heron can be found along the Colorado River and its tributaries, while birds of prey like the red-tailed hawk and golden eagle patrol the skies in search of prey.

The Grand Canyon also supports a variety of amphibians, although their numbers are fewer due to the region's arid climate. Amphibians such as the canyon tree frog and the red-spotted toad can be found in the canyon's wetter areas, particularly near springs, streams, and seeps. These small, hardy creatures have adapted to the canyon's fluctuating temperatures and water availability, often estivating (a form of dormancy) during the hottest and driest periods of the year.

The invertebrate population of the Grand Canyon is equally diverse, including butterflies, beetles, ants, and bees. These small creatures play essential roles in the canyon's ecosystem, from pollinating plants to decomposing organic matter. Butterflies, in particular, are a common sight during the warmer months, with species like the painted lady and monarch adding splashes of color to the canyon's rugged landscape.

The flora and fauna of the Grand Canyon form a delicate web of life, each species playing a vital role in the ecosystem's overall health. From the predators at the top of the food chain to the tiniest invertebrates, the wildlife of the Grand Canyon has adapted to survive in one of the most unique and challenging environments on Earth. As we explore the canyon's diverse ecosystems, we are reminded of the importance of preserving this natural wonder and its inhabitants for future generations to experience and enjoy. The Grand Canyon's wildlife is a testament to the resilience of nature, a living legacy of adaptation, survival, and the incredible diversity of life that inhabits our planet.

Chapter 6: The Plants that Thrive in the Grand Canyon

The Grand Canyon, one of the most awe-inspiring natural wonders in the world, is not only a geological marvel but also a biological treasure trove filled with an astonishing variety of plant life. Stretching over 277 miles in length, this immense chasm created by the Colorado River harbors a wide range of ecosystems, each supporting distinct types of plants that have adapted to the canyon's challenging and diverse environments. From the arid desert floors to the cool, forested plateaus of the higher rims, the plant life of the Grand Canyon reflects the extremes of climate, elevation, and terrain found within its borders. The canyon's dramatic elevation changes, which range from about 2,000 feet above sea level along the Colorado River to over 8,000 feet on the North Rim, create a series of microclimates that support everything from hardy desert plants to towering conifers. Each plant species, whether it be a tough, sun-loving cactus or a shade-seeking fern, plays a critical role in the canyon's complex ecosystems.

Starting from the bottom of the canyon near the Colorado River, where the environment is dry, hot, and dominated by rocky cliffs and sandy expanses, one finds plant species that are well-suited to the harsh conditions of the desert. Cacti are among the most iconic and important plants in this lower region. The prickly pear cactus is one of the most recognizable, with its flat, paddle-shaped pads that are covered in spines. This cactus has evolved to store water in its fleshy tissues, allowing it to survive long periods without rainfall. Its bright yellow or orange flowers, which bloom in the spring, add a splash of color to the otherwise stark landscape, and its fruit, called tunas, are edible and provide a source of nutrition for both wildlife and humans. The prickly pear is a resilient survivor of the desert, enduring extreme temperatures that can fluctuate between scorching daytime heat and cool nighttime lows.

The saguaro cactus, another iconic desert plant, can also be found in the Grand Canyon, although it is more common in lower elevations to the south of the park. The saguaro is the largest cactus in the United States, capable of growing over 40 feet tall. Its towering, branching arms and thick, ribbed trunk allow it to store vast amounts of water during rare rainfalls, which it uses to survive long, dry periods. While it grows slowly, the saguaro can live for over 150 years, making it a symbol of endurance and longevity in the desert. The plant's small white flowers, which bloom in late spring and early summer, are an important food source for bees, bats, and birds like the Gila woodpecker and the cactus wren, which also use the saguaro as a nesting site.

In addition to cacti, many other plants thrive in the lower elevations of the Grand Canyon, where drought tolerance is key to survival. Creosote bushes are one of the most common plants in the desert scrub habitat. These hardy shrubs, with their small, waxy leaves, are well adapted to arid environments. Their leaves help conserve water by reducing evaporation, and their deep root systems allow them to access water far below the surface. The creosote bush is known for its distinctive smell, often compared to the scent of rain in the desert, and it has long been used by indigenous peoples for medicinal purposes.

Another important desert plant is the ocotillo, a tall, spindly shrub that looks almost like a cluster of thorny sticks rising from the ground. Though it appears dead and leafless for much of the year, the ocotillo springs to life after rains, quickly growing small green leaves and producing bright red, tubular flowers at the tips of its branches. These flowers are a vital nectar source for hummingbirds, particularly during migration periods. Like many desert plants, the ocotillo has evolved to conserve water by shedding its leaves during dry periods and regrowing them only when conditions improve.

As one ascends from the canyon's floor to the mid-elevations, the plant communities begin to change, reflecting cooler temperatures and slightly more rainfall. Here, in the semi-arid zones, desert grasslands and scrublands dominate, with a variety of grasses, shrubs, and wildflowers dotting the landscape. Sagebrush is a common sight in these areas, its silvery-green leaves and distinctive smell making it easy to identify. Sagebrush is an important plant for both wildlife and indigenous peoples; it provides food for animals like mule deer and serves as a medicinal plant for many Native American tribes. Another common shrub in the mid-elevations is the cliffrose, which produces fragrant yellow and white flowers in the spring. The cliffrose has a deep root system that allows it to thrive on rocky slopes and in poor soil, and its seeds are dispersed by the wind, helping it colonize new areas.

Junipers and pinyon pines also begin to appear in these mid-elevations, forming open woodlands known as pinyon-juniper forests. The pinyon pine is particularly important to the ecosystem, as its seeds, known as pine nuts, provide a critical food source for many animals, including birds, rodents, and even humans. Native peoples of the region have harvested pine nuts for thousands of years, using them as a staple food in their diets. The juniper, with its twisted, gnarled branches and small blue berries, is another key species in these woodlands. Its dense wood is highly resistant to decay, making it useful for building materials, and its berries are eaten by birds and small mammals.

Continuing upward to the higher elevations, particularly on the North Rim, the landscape transitions once again, this time to a more temperate forest environment dominated by ponderosa pines, Douglas firs, and aspens. The North Rim of the Grand Canyon is significantly cooler and receives more precipitation than the lower elevations, allowing these large coniferous trees to thrive. The ponderosa pine, with its tall, straight trunk and distinctive orange-brown bark, is one of the most common and important trees in the canyon's high-elevation forests. These pines can grow over 200 feet tall and live for hundreds of years, providing habitat for a wide range of wildlife, including birds, squirrels, and insects. Their thick bark helps protect them from fire, which is a natural part of the forest ecosystem in the Grand Canyon. Fire helps clear out underbrush and allows new seedlings to grow, maintaining the health and diversity of the forest.

The Douglas fir is another towering conifer found in the higher elevations of the Grand Canyon. These trees are known for their soft, flat needles and their cones, which have distinctive three-pointed bracts. Douglas firs are fast-growing and can reach great heights, providing important habitat for species like the Kaibab squirrel, a unique subspecies found only in the ponderosa pine forests of the North Rim. This squirrel has a distinctive tufted tail and relies on the seeds of ponderosa pines and Douglas firs for food. Aspens, with their bright green leaves that turn golden in the fall, add a splash of color to the forests of the North Rim. These trees grow in dense stands, often sprouting from the same root system, which allows them to quickly regenerate after disturbances like fire or logging.

In addition to trees, the higher elevations of the Grand Canyon support a wide variety of wildflowers, ferns, and other plants that thrive in cooler, moister conditions. Lupines, paintbrushes, and columbines are just a few of the many wildflowers that bloom in the spring and summer, adding bursts of color to the forest floor. These flowers attract pollinators like bees, butterflies, and hummingbirds, which play a critical role in the reproduction of plants in the canyon's ecosystems.

Throughout the Grand Canyon, from the desert floors to the forested rims, plants have adapted to survive in one of the most extreme and varied environments on Earth. Their strategies for survival include deep root systems, water-storing tissues, and the ability to thrive in poor, rocky soils. These adaptations not only allow the plants to survive but also support the diverse array of wildlife that depends on them for food, shelter, and habitat. The plants of the Grand Canyon are a testament to the resilience and ingenuity of life in the face of harsh and ever-changing conditions.

Beyond their ecological importance, the plants of the Grand Canyon also have deep cultural significance. For thousands of years, indigenous peoples have lived in and around the canyon, using the plants for food, medicine, tools, and spiritual practices. The Havasupai, Hopi, Navajo, and other tribes have a profound connection to the land and its plants, which they see as gifts from the Earth. Many of the plants in the canyon, such as the pinyon pine, juniper, and various medicinal herbs, continue to be used by Native peoples in traditional practices today.

As we explore the Grand Canyon and marvel at its geological wonders, it's important to remember the intricate and interconnected web of life that exists within its walls. The plants that thrive in the Grand Canyon, from the smallest wildflower to the tallest pine, are vital components of the canyon's ecosystems, supporting a rich diversity of wildlife and playing a crucial role in the health of this natural wonder. Their ability to adapt and survive in such a challenging environment is a testament to the resilience of nature and a reminder of the importance of preserving these unique and fragile ecosystems for future generations to enjoy and study.

Chapter 7: The Grand Canyon's Native Tribes

The Grand Canyon is not only a natural wonder but also a place steeped in human history, where ancient cultures and Native American tribes have lived, thrived, and developed deep connections to the land for thousands of years. Long before it became a national park and a popular tourist destination, the Grand Canyon was home to several Native tribes who adapted to the diverse and sometimes harsh environments of the canyon. These tribes have left an indelible mark on the area, and their stories, traditions, and ways of life are inextricably tied to the canyon's landscape. Their history reflects both a deep reverence for the land and a struggle for survival in one of North America's most unique and challenging terrains. Today, the descendants of these tribes continue to live in and around the Grand Canyon, maintaining their cultural heritage while preserving their sacred connection to this vast and beautiful place.

The Havasupai, the Hopi, the Hualapai, the Navajo, the Zuni, and the Southern Paiute are some of the most notable tribes that have called the Grand Canyon and its surrounding areas home. Each of these tribes has its own unique history, cultural practices, and relationship with the canyon, yet they all share a deep respect for the land and its resources. Their lives were shaped by the canyon's dramatic landscape, which influenced their social structures, economies, religious beliefs, and daily survival.

The Havasupai Tribe, often referred to as the "People of the Blue-Green Waters," is one of the most well-known tribes associated with the Grand Canyon. The Havasupai have lived in and around the canyon for at least 800 years, although archaeological evidence suggests their ancestors may have inhabited the area for much longer. Their name comes from the stunning blue-green waters of Havasu Creek, which runs through their homeland in the western part of the canyon. The Havasupai were originally a semi-nomadic people, following a seasonal cycle of hunting, gathering, and farming. During the spring and summer, they lived in the cooler, higher elevations of the plateau, where they planted crops like corn, beans, and squash. In the fall and winter, they moved down into the warmer, more sheltered areas of the canyon, where they harvested wild plants and hunted game.

Havasupai culture is deeply connected to the natural environment, particularly the waters of Havasu Creek, which provide life-sustaining resources in the otherwise arid desert. The Havasupai people have traditionally relied on the creek for drinking water, irrigation, and fishing. The waterfalls along Havasu Creek, including the famous Havasu Falls, are considered sacred by the Havasupai, and their vibrant turquoise waters are a symbol of the tribe's enduring connection to the land. For centuries, the Havasupai lived in relative isolation in the Grand Canyon, but the arrival of European settlers and the expansion of the United States in the 19th century brought significant changes to their way of life. In 1882, much of the Havasupai's ancestral land was taken from them when the federal government created the Grand Canyon Forest Reserve, later to become the Grand Canyon National Park. The Havasupai were confined to a small reservation in Havasu Canyon, but they continued to fight for the return of their land. In 1975, after years of legal battles, the U.S. government restored over 185,000 acres of their ancestral land to the Havasupai, allowing them to continue their traditional practices and live in their sacred homeland.

The Hopi Tribe, another prominent group associated with the Grand Canyon, has a history that stretches back thousands of years. The Hopi people trace their origins to ancient Puebloan cultures that once inhabited the Four Corners region, including the area that is now the Grand Canyon. The Hopi have a unique worldview centered on their relationship with the land, the cosmos, and their spiritual deities, known as kachinas. For the Hopi, the Grand Canyon is not just a physical place but a sacred site that plays a central role in their creation story. According to Hopi tradition, the Grand Canyon is the place where their ancestors emerged from the underground world into the present world, a journey that was guided by spiritual forces. The canyon's deep gorges and towering cliffs are seen as portals to the spiritual realms, and certain areas within the canyon are considered sacred ground where important religious ceremonies are held.

The Hopi people are known for their advanced agricultural practices, particularly their ability to grow crops in the arid desert environment of the Colorado Plateau. Using dry farming techniques, the Hopi have cultivated corn, beans, and squash for centuries, relying on careful water management and deep knowledge of the land to sustain their crops. The Hopi also engage in intricate weaving, pottery making, and other traditional crafts, many of which are tied to their religious and ceremonial life. Despite the challenges of colonization and land loss, the Hopi people have maintained their cultural identity and continue to practice their spiritual traditions today.

The Hualapai Tribe, whose name means "People of the Tall Pines," also has a long history in the Grand Canyon region. The Hualapai traditionally lived in the southern and western parts of the canyon, where they hunted, gathered wild plants, and farmed along the rivers and streams. The Hualapai people were semi-nomadic, moving between the canyon floor and the surrounding plateaus depending on the season. Like the Havasupai, the Hualapai developed a deep understanding of the canyon's ecosystems and were adept at surviving in the harsh desert environment. They hunted animals such as deer, bighorn sheep, and rabbits, and gathered plants like agave, mesquite beans, and piñon nuts, which provided vital food sources.

In the 19th century, the arrival of European settlers and the construction of the transcontinental railroad disrupted the traditional way of life for the Hualapai. Many Hualapai were forced off their land, and the tribe's population was decimated by disease, warfare, and displacement. In 1883, the U.S. government established the Hualapai Indian Reservation, which includes parts of the Grand Canyon's western rim. Despite these challenges, the Hualapai people have persevered, and today they continue to live on their reservation and maintain their cultural traditions. The Hualapai are perhaps best known today for their stewardship of Grand Canyon West, a popular tourist destination that includes the famous Skywalk, a glass bridge that extends over the edge of the canyon.

The Navajo Nation, the largest Native American tribe in the United States, also has a significant presence in the Grand Canyon region. The Navajo people, known as the Diné, have a long and complex history that includes migration, adaptation, and resistance to outside forces. The Navajo arrived in the Southwest around 1,000 years ago, and over time, they developed a pastoral lifestyle based on sheep herding, farming, and weaving. The Navajo's vast homeland, known as Dinétah, stretches across parts of Arizona, New Mexico, Utah, and Colorado, and includes areas near the Grand Canyon. While the Navajo did not traditionally live within the canyon itself, they have long considered the area to be part of their spiritual homeland.

The Navajo people have a deep connection to the land and view it as a living being with which they share a reciprocal relationship. According to Navajo beliefs, the Earth is their Mother, and they have a responsibility to care for the land and ensure its health for future generations. The Navajo have numerous sacred sites within and around the Grand Canyon, including the San Francisco Peaks, which are believed to be the home of spiritual deities. Traditional Navajo ceremonies, songs, and prayers often reference the canyon and its natural features, reinforcing the tribe's spiritual connection to the land.

The Zuni Tribe, another Puebloan people, also has historical and spiritual ties to the Grand Canyon. The Zuni, like the Hopi, believe that the canyon is a place of emergence, where their ancestors entered the world. The Zuni have long lived in the region to the south of the Grand Canyon, and their culture is deeply rooted in agriculture, particularly the cultivation of corn. The Zuni are known for their elaborate religious ceremonies, which often involve the use of kachinas—spiritual beings that represent the forces of nature and the ancestors. These ceremonies are performed to ensure the fertility of the land, the health of the community, and the balance of the natural world.

The Southern Paiute people have traditionally inhabited the northern regions of the Grand Canyon, as well as parts of Utah, Nevada, and California. The Southern Paiute have a deep connection to the canyon, which they call "Kaibab" in their language. The Paiute people were hunter-gatherers who lived in small, mobile bands and relied on the canyon's diverse ecosystems for food, water, and shelter. They gathered plants like pinyon nuts, yucca, and wild onions, and hunted animals such as rabbits, deer, and bighorn sheep. The Southern Paiute also have a rich spiritual tradition, and certain areas of the Grand Canyon are considered sacred to them. They believe that the canyon is home to powerful spirits, and they have long performed rituals and ceremonies to honor these spirits and seek their guidance.

Despite the profound connections that Native American tribes have to the Grand Canyon, the arrival of European settlers and the establishment of the national park in 1919 dramatically altered the lives of these indigenous peoples. Many tribes were forcibly removed from their ancestral lands, and their traditional ways of life were disrupted by the influx of tourists, miners, and ranchers. The creation of the Grand Canyon National Park further restricted Native access to the canyon, as federal authorities sought to preserve the area for recreation and scientific study, often at the expense of indigenous peoples' rights and cultural practices.

In recent years, there has been a growing recognition of the importance of Native American perspectives in the stewardship of the

Grand Canyon. Many tribes, including the Havasupai, Hualapai, Hopi, Navajo, and Southern Paiute, have been involved in efforts to preserve their cultural heritage and protect the canyon's sacred sites. Some tribes have partnered with the National Park Service to co-manage certain areas of the canyon, while others have developed their own initiatives to promote sustainable tourism and educate visitors about their history and traditions. For example, the Hualapai Tribe's Grand Canyon West project has become a major tourist attraction, offering visitors a chance to learn about Hualapai culture while enjoying breathtaking views of the canyon.

The Grand Canyon's Native tribes continue to play a vital role in the story of the canyon, offering a perspective that goes beyond the geological wonder to encompass a deep, spiritual connection to the land. Their histories, traditions, and struggles serve as a reminder that the Grand Canyon is not just a natural monument but a living, cultural landscape shaped by millennia of human experience. As more efforts are made to honor and include Native voices in the management and interpretation of the Grand Canyon, visitors are gaining a fuller understanding of the canyon's significance—not just as a breathtaking landscape but as a sacred place with deep cultural and historical meaning.

Chapter 8: Grand Canyon National Park Adventures

Grand Canyon National Park is a sprawling natural wonder that offers a wide array of adventures for visitors of all ages and interests. From the moment you step foot inside the park, the sheer scale of the canyon takes your breath away, with its towering cliffs, deep gorges, and striking vistas stretching as far as the eye can see. But beyond simply admiring the view, Grand Canyon National Park is a playground for adventurers, where each day can bring a new experience, from hiking rugged trails to rafting along the mighty Colorado River. Whether you're a seasoned explorer looking for a challenge or a family seeking an unforgettable outdoor adventure, the park has something for everyone.

One of the most popular ways to experience the Grand Canyon is by hiking its many trails, which vary in difficulty from easy, scenic walks along the rim to strenuous, multi-day treks into the canyon's depths. The South Rim, which is the most visited part of the park, offers a variety of well-maintained trails with breathtaking overlooks and opportunities to spot wildlife. One of the most iconic hikes is the Bright Angel Trail, a challenging but rewarding journey that descends into the canyon, offering spectacular views at every turn. The trail is steep and can be difficult, especially in the heat of summer, but those who venture down are rewarded with a sense of the canyon's immense size and grandeur that can't be fully appreciated from the rim alone. Along the way, hikers can stop at rest houses, campgrounds, and even Indian Garden, a lush oasis nestled deep within the canyon.

For those seeking a less demanding hike, the Rim Trail offers a more leisurely way to explore the South Rim, with paved pathways and stunning views of the canyon's many layers. Stretching from the South Kaibab Trailhead to Hermit's Rest, the Rim Trail allows visitors to enjoy the beauty of the Grand Canyon without the physical demands of descending into the canyon itself. The trail is accessible to people of all fitness levels and provides numerous lookout points where you can stop, take in the views, and learn about the geology and history of the area through interpretive signs.

Another popular hiking destination is the North Rim, which sees far fewer visitors than the South Rim and offers a more remote, wilderness experience. The North Rim is only open from mid-May to mid-October due to heavy snowfall in the winter months, but during the summer, it provides a cooler, more tranquil alternative to the busier South Rim. Here, hikers can explore the North Kaibab Trail, which descends into the canyon from the forested plateau above, or venture out to Point Imperial or Cape Royal for sweeping vistas of the canyon and the surrounding landscape. The North Rim is also home to several backcountry trails that take hikers deep into the wilderness, where they can experience the solitude and beauty of the Grand Canyon away from the crowds.

Beyond hiking, one of the most exhilarating ways to experience the Grand Canyon is by rafting the Colorado River. The river, which carved the canyon over millions of years, flows through the heart of the park and offers a unique perspective on the canyon's sheer size and power. Rafting trips range from short half-day excursions to multi-day adventures that take you deep into the canyon, where you'll navigate rapids, camp along the riverbanks, and explore hidden side canyons and waterfalls. For those seeking an adrenaline rush, whitewater rafting trips through the Grand Canyon's famous rapids, such as Lava Falls and Crystal Rapids, provide a thrilling ride, while calmer sections of the river offer a more relaxed, scenic float.

For many, a rafting trip down the Colorado River is the ultimate Grand Canyon adventure, as it allows you to experience the canyon from a completely different vantage point. From the river, the canyon's towering walls rise dramatically above you, creating a sense of awe and wonder that is hard to match. Along the way, you'll encounter a variety of landscapes, from narrow, twisting canyons to wide, open stretches of river, and you'll have the opportunity to spot wildlife, including bighorn sheep, river otters, and a wide array of bird species. Many guided rafting trips also include stops at historic sites, such as ancient Native American dwellings and rock art, providing a glimpse into the canyon's rich cultural history.

For those who prefer to stay on solid ground but still want an adventure, mule rides offer a unique way to explore the Grand Canyon. Mules have been used to traverse the canyon's steep, narrow trails for over a century, and today, visitors can take guided mule rides along some of the park's most famous routes. One of the most popular mule rides is the journey down the Bright Angel Trail to Phantom Ranch, a rustic lodge located at the bottom of the canyon. The ride is a thrilling experience, as the sure-footed mules carefully navigate the steep switchbacks and narrow ledges of the trail, offering riders a close-up view of the canyon's incredible rock formations. For those who prefer a shorter trip, there are also mule rides along the rim, where you can enjoy panoramic views of the canyon without descending into its depths.

If you're looking for a more relaxed way to explore the Grand Canyon, scenic drives offer an excellent option. The Desert View Drive, which runs along the South Rim from Grand Canyon Village to the Desert View Watchtower, is one of the most popular routes. Along the way, you'll pass several overlooks that offer stunning views of the canyon and the Colorado River far below. The drive also provides access to some of the park's most significant cultural and historical sites, including the Tusayan Ruin and Museum, where you can learn about the ancient Puebloan people who once lived in the area. At the eastern end of the drive, the Desert View Watchtower, designed by architect Mary Colter, offers a panoramic view of the Grand Canyon and the Painted Desert beyond.

Another scenic drive is the Hermit Road, which runs west from Grand Canyon Village to Hermit's Rest. This road is closed to private vehicles for most of the year, but a free shuttle bus provides easy access to the many overlooks and trailheads along the way. Stops along the Hermit Road include Maricopa Point, Hopi Point, and Pima Point, each offering a different perspective on the canyon's vast landscape. At the end of the road, Hermit's Rest, another of Mary Colter's architectural creations, provides a peaceful spot to relax and take in the views.

For those interested in the history and culture of the Grand Canyon, the park offers several opportunities to learn about the Native American tribes that have lived in the area for centuries. The Grand Canyon Village area includes the Hopi House, an adobe-style building designed by Mary Colter in the early 20th century. The Hopi House showcases traditional Native American arts and crafts, including pottery, weaving, and jewelry, and offers visitors a chance to learn about the culture and traditions of the Hopi people. Nearby, the Yavapai Geology Museum provides an in-depth look at the geological forces that shaped the Grand Canyon, with exhibits on the canyon's rock layers, fossils, and ancient landscapes.

For families, the Grand Canyon offers a range of kid-friendly activities that combine adventure with education. The park's Junior Ranger Program allows children to earn a Junior Ranger badge by completing a series of activities and learning about the park's natural and cultural history. Kids can participate in ranger-led programs, such as guided walks, talks, and campfire programs, where they can learn about the canyon's wildlife, geology, and history in a fun and engaging way. The park also offers several family-friendly hikes, including the Trail of Time, a paved, interpretive trail along the South Rim that explains the geological history of the Grand Canyon through interactive exhibits and displays.

For a truly unforgettable experience, visitors can take to the skies with a helicopter or airplane tour of the Grand Canyon. These aerial tours provide a bird's-eye view of the canyon's vast expanse, allowing you to see areas that are inaccessible by foot or road. From above, you'll get a sense of the sheer scale of the canyon, as well as its intricate network of cliffs, mesas, and valleys. Many tours also fly over the remote North Rim, offering a glimpse of the canyon's more rugged and less-visited areas.

In the winter months, the Grand Canyon takes on a whole new character, with snow blanketing the rim and adding a layer of serene beauty to the landscape. While some areas of the park, such as the North Rim, are closed due to snow, the South Rim remains open year-round, offering a quieter, more peaceful experience. Winter visitors can enjoy hiking, wildlife watching, and even snowshoeing along the rim trails, as well as cozying up in the historic lodges that dot the South Rim.

For those seeking a more immersive adventure, backpacking trips into the Grand Canyon's backcountry offer the chance to explore the park's most remote and untouched areas. Backpackers can follow established trails, such as the Tonto Trail, which runs along a plateau above the river, or venture into lesser-known areas where solitude and stunning scenery abound. Backcountry permits are required for overnight trips, and preparation is key, as the canyon's rugged terrain and extreme weather conditions can make backpacking a challenging but rewarding experience.

In addition to its many outdoor adventures, Grand Canyon National Park is also a place for quiet reflection and awe-inspiring moments. Watching the sunrise or sunset over the canyon is an experience that stays with visitors long after they've left the park. The colors of the canyon walls shift and change with the light, creating a stunning palette of reds, oranges, purples, and blues. Some of the best spots for watching the sunrise or sunset include Mather Point, Yaki

behind sediment that would eventually form the colorful rocks we see today.

The Redwall Limestone, which sits beneath the Supai Group, is another major contributor to the Grand Canyon's fiery color palette. Despite its name, the Redwall Limestone is actually a grayish-blue rock, but its surfaces are often stained red by the iron-rich sediments that have washed down from the layers above. This staining gives the Redwall Limestone its distinctive reddish hue when viewed from afar. The Redwall Limestone formed in a shallow, tropical sea that covered the region around 340 million years ago, during the Mississippian period. The clear, warm waters of this ancient sea were home to a variety of marine life, including corals, brachiopods, and crinoids, whose skeletal remains contributed to the formation of the limestone. Over time, these marine deposits were compacted and cemented into solid rock, creating the massive cliffs of limestone that now form one of the most visually striking layers in the canyon.

Below the Redwall Limestone is another set of rock layers that contribute to the Grand Canyon's colorful geology. The Muav Limestone, Bright Angel Shale, and Tapeats Sandstone form what is known as the Tonto Group, which dates back to the Cambrian period, around 500 million years ago. These layers are particularly rich in earthy tones of green, gray, and purple. The greenish hues of the Bright Angel Shale, for example, come from the presence of minerals like glauconite, which forms in shallow marine environments. The Bright Angel Shale was deposited in a coastal environment, where ancient seas advanced and retreated over millions of years, leaving behind layers of mud and clay that would eventually become shale. The grayish-purple tones of the Muav Limestone, meanwhile, are the result of the presence of magnesium and other minerals that formed in the shallow, warm seas of the Cambrian period.

One of the most ancient and visually stunning rock formations in the Grand Canyon is the Vishnu Schist, which forms the dark, jagged cliffs at the bottom of the canyon. The Vishnu Schist is nearly two billion years old, making it some of the oldest exposed rock on the planet. It formed deep beneath the Earth's surface, where intense heat and pressure transformed older sedimentary and volcanic rocks into the dark, crystalline schist we see today. The Vishnu Schist is characterized by its deep shades of black, gray, and brown, which provide a striking contrast to the brighter colors of the younger rock layers above. The Vishnu Schist, along with the Zoroaster Granite, which intruded into the schist around 1.7 billion years ago, forms the "basement" of the Grand Canyon, representing the ancient roots of the Earth's crust.

The contrast between the Vishnu Schist and the overlying rock layers is one of the most dramatic features of the Grand Canyon, highlighting the immense geological time scales involved in its formation. Above the Vishnu Schist lies the Great Unconformity, a geological boundary that represents a gap of hundreds of millions of years in the rock record. This unconformity marks a period of uplift and erosion that occurred during the Precambrian era, when the ancient mountains that once stood in the region were eroded away, leaving behind a flat surface. This surface was later covered by sedimentary rocks, including the Tapeats Sandstone, which began to form around 525 million years ago. The Tapeats Sandstone, with its warm, golden hues, is one of the most recognizable layers in the Grand Canyon, and it marks the beginning of a new chapter in the region's geological history.

The Tapeats Sandstone, along with the other layers of the Tonto Group, was deposited in a shallow sea that once covered the area during the Cambrian period. The sandstone is composed primarily of quartz grains, which give it its light, sandy color. As the sea advanced and retreated over millions of years, layers of sand were deposited and compacted into sandstone, creating the thick, horizontal bands that can be seen in the canyon walls today. The bright, golden color of the Tapeats Sandstone contrasts sharply with the darker Vishnu Schist below, providing a vivid example of how different geological processes can produce strikingly different rock formations and colors.

As you move upward through the layers of the Grand Canyon, you encounter the Kaibab Limestone, which forms the caprock of the canyon and is responsible for the bright, light-colored cliffs that define the rim. The Kaibab Limestone was deposited around 270 million years ago, during the Permian period, in a shallow, tropical sea. The limestone is rich in fossils, including brachiopods, crinoids, and sponges, which provide evidence of the marine environment that once existed in the region. The Kaibab Limestone is typically a light gray or buff color, but it can appear almost white in certain lighting conditions, creating a stark contrast with the darker layers below. This light-colored rock reflects sunlight, giving the canyon's rim a luminous quality, especially during sunrise and sunset when the low angle of the sun enhances the play of light and shadow across the landscape.

The interplay of light and color in the Grand Canyon is one of the most captivating aspects of its geology. As the sun moves across the sky, the colors of the canyon shift and change, creating a dynamic and ever-changing landscape. In the early morning and late afternoon, when the sun is low on the horizon, the reds, oranges, and purples of the canyon walls are especially vivid, as the warm light enhances the natural hues of the rocks. At midday, when the sun is directly overhead, the colors can appear more muted, with the canyon taking on a more uniform, earthy tone. Clouds, storms, and seasonal changes also play a role in the canyon's color palette, with the rich hues of the rocks sometimes appearing more subdued on overcast days or during the winter months when snow blankets the rim.

The geology behind the Grand Canyon's colors is not just a matter of aesthetics—it also provides valuable insights into the processes that shaped the landscape. Each layer of rock tells a story about the Earth's past, from ancient seas and coastal plains to volcanic eruptions and mountain-building events. By studying the colors, composition, and structure of these rocks, geologists can reconstruct the history of the region, tracing the evolution of the landscape over nearly two billion years. The colors of the Grand Canyon are a visual record of the Earth's geological processes, offering a glimpse into the forces that have shaped our planet over vast stretches of time.

In addition to their geological significance, the colors of the Grand Canyon have played a cultural role as well. For thousands of years, Native American tribes have lived in and around the canyon, drawing inspiration from its vibrant hues and dramatic landscapes. The Hopi, Havasupai, Navajo, and other tribes have incorporated the colors of the canyon into their art, pottery, and textiles, using the natural pigments of the rocks to create dyes and paints. For these tribes, the colors of the Grand Canyon are not just a geological curiosity—they are a reflection of the spiritual and cultural significance of the land.

In conclusion, the geology behind the Grand Canyon's colors is a complex and fascinating story that spans nearly two billion years of Earth's history. From the deep reds and oranges of the Supai Group to the cool greens and purples of the Bright Angel Shale, each layer of rock represents a different environment, a different process, and a different period of time. The interplay of light and color across the canyon walls creates a dynamic, ever-changing landscape that is as captivating as it is awe-inspiring. Whether you're gazing at the canyon from the rim or exploring its depths, the colors of the Grand Canyon are a reminder of the powerful geological forces that have shaped our planet and continue to shape it today.

Chapter 10: The Grand Canyon's Fossils & Ancient Creatures

The Grand Canyon is not only an awe-inspiring natural wonder of immense beauty and scale, but it is also a time capsule of Earth's deep past, containing some of the most fascinating fossils and remnants of ancient creatures that ever roamed the planet. Stretching across nearly 277 miles, the Grand Canyon provides an unparalleled window into the history of life on Earth, revealing evidence of life forms that existed hundreds of millions of years ago, long before humans ever set foot on the planet. The layers of rock exposed within the canyon walls serve as a kind of geological library, recording the evolution of life through fossils that have been preserved in sedimentary formations. Each rock layer tells a different story, and by examining these fossils, scientists can piece together the rich history of ancient ecosystems, the species that inhabited them, and the dramatic changes in climate and geography that shaped the environment over eons. The Grand Canyon's fossils offer a glimpse into an ancient world, one filled with strange and fascinating creatures that are long extinct but continue to inspire curiosity and wonder.

The story of the Grand Canyon's fossils begins deep in the canyon's lower rock layers, which are among the oldest exposed rocks on Earth. These layers, including the Vishnu Schist and Zoroaster Granite, date back nearly two billion years to the Precambrian era. However, despite the immense age of these rocks, fossils are rare in these lower layers, primarily because they were formed during a time when life on Earth was still in its earliest stages. Most of the rock layers that make up the basement of the canyon are metamorphic and igneous, meaning they were formed through intense heat and pressure, conditions that are not conducive to the preservation of fossils. At this point in Earth's history, life was mostly microscopic, consisting of single-celled organisms like bacteria and algae that left behind few, if any, fossils.

As we move upward through the layers of the canyon, we encounter rock formations from the Cambrian period, around 540 million years ago, when life on Earth began to explode in diversity. This period is known as the "Cambrian Explosion," a time when many major groups of animals first appeared in the fossil record. The rock layers of the Tonto Group, which include the Tapeats Sandstone, Bright Angel Shale, and Muav Limestone, are especially rich in fossils from this era. These fossils provide a detailed record of the marine life that once thrived in the shallow seas that covered the region during the Cambrian period. The oceans of this time were teeming with a wide variety of invertebrate life, including trilobites, brachiopods, and mollusks, whose fossilized remains are still visible in the canyon's rock layers today.

Trilobites are among the most common and iconic fossils found in the Grand Canyon, particularly in the Cambrian-aged rock layers. These extinct marine arthropods resembled large, segmented insects and lived on the seafloor, scavenging for food and burrowing into the sediment. Trilobites were highly successful creatures that existed for nearly 270 million years, and their fossils are found in many locations around the world. In the Grand Canyon, trilobite fossils are often found in the Bright Angel Shale, where the fine-grained mudstone and siltstone helped preserve these ancient creatures in remarkable detail. Some trilobite fossils are so well-preserved that you can still see the intricate patterns on their exoskeletons, providing a window into the anatomy and lifestyle of these long-extinct animals.

In addition to trilobites, the Bright Angel Shale and other Cambrian rock layers are home to fossils of brachiopods, crinoids, and other marine invertebrates. Brachiopods are shellfish that resemble clams but belong to a completely different group of animals. They were abundant in the seas of the Cambrian period and are often found as fossilized shells in the limestone and shale of the Grand Canyon. Crinoids, also known as "sea lilies," are another common fossil in the canyon. Although they resemble plants, crinoids are actually animals related to starfish and sea urchins. They anchored themselves to the seafloor with long, stem-like structures and used their feathery arms to capture food particles from the water. Fossilized crinoid stems are frequently found in the Muav Limestone, where they often appear as small, circular or star-shaped disks.

Moving up through the canyon's rock layers, we reach the Devonian and Mississippian periods, around 400 to 320 million years ago, when marine life continued to thrive in the warm, shallow seas that covered the region. The Temple Butte Limestone and Redwall Limestone, which were deposited during this time, contain an abundance of marine fossils, including corals, brachiopods, and bryozoans. Corals, in particular, were widespread during the Devonian period, and fossilized coral reefs can still be seen in the Redwall Limestone. These ancient reefs were home to a diverse array of marine life, much like modern coral reefs today, providing shelter and food for countless species. The fossilized remains of these reefs offer valuable insights into the marine ecosystems of the past, revealing the complex interactions between species and the environmental conditions that shaped their development.

One of the most impressive fossils found in the Redwall Limestone is the remains of large marine animals, such as sharks and fish. During the Mississippian period, the seas that covered the Grand Canyon were home to a variety of fish, including early sharks. Fossilized teeth and spines from these ancient predators have been found in the Redwall Limestone, providing evidence of their presence in the region. These fossils offer a glimpse into the world of early vertebrates and the evolutionary transition from simple, jawless fish to more complex, predatory species. The discovery of shark fossils in the Grand Canyon adds another layer of intrigue to the canyon's fossil record, showing that even in ancient times, the region was home to some of the most formidable creatures in the ocean.

As we continue upward through the canyon's rock layers, we reach the Permian period, around 300 to 250 million years ago, when the seas that once covered the region began to retreat. During this time, the environment transitioned from a shallow marine setting to a more arid, desert-like landscape. The Coconino Sandstone, Hermit Shale, and Kaibab Limestone, which were deposited during the Permian period, contain fossils that reflect this changing environment. The Coconino Sandstone, for example, is famous for its fossilized sand dunes and the tracks of ancient reptiles that once roamed the desert. These fossilized footprints, known as ichnofossils, provide a rare glimpse into the behavior of these early land animals, showing how they moved across the sand dunes in search of food or shelter. The tracks preserved in the Coconino Sandstone are some of the best examples of fossilized footprints in the world, offering a fascinating record of life during the Permian period.

In addition to reptile tracks, the Kaibab Limestone contains fossils of marine organisms that lived in the shallow seas that briefly returned to the region during the late Permian period. These fossils include brachiopods, mollusks, and bryozoans, as well as the remains of marine reptiles like ichthyosaurs and plesiosaurs. The presence of these marine fossils in the Kaibab Limestone shows that even as the environment became more arid, the region continued to experience periods of marine inundation, creating a dynamic and ever-changing landscape.

The Grand Canyon's fossil record comes to an end in the uppermost rock layers, which were deposited during the Triassic and Jurassic periods, around 250 to 150 million years ago. Although these rock layers are not as well-preserved in the Grand Canyon as they are in other parts of the Southwest, they still contain evidence of ancient ecosystems, including the footprints of early dinosaurs. These tracks, along with the fossils of plants and other organisms, provide a tantalizing glimpse into the world of the Mesozoic era, when dinosaurs ruled the Earth.

In conclusion, the Grand Canyon's fossils and ancient creatures offer a remarkable journey through time, revealing the history of life on Earth over nearly two billion years. From the microscopic organisms of the Precambrian era to the marine invertebrates of the Cambrian seas, the fossils preserved in the canyon's rock layers provide a detailed record of the evolution of life, showing how species adapted to changing environments and how ecosystems evolved over time. The discovery of trilobites, crinoids, brachiopods, sharks, and even early reptiles and dinosaurs in the Grand Canyon is a testament to the rich and diverse history of life that once thrived in the region. These fossils not only help us understand the geological processes that shaped the canyon, but they also offer a glimpse into the ancient world, a world filled with strange and fascinating creatures that continue to captivate our imagination today. As scientists continue to study the Grand Canyon's fossils, they are uncovering new insights into the history of life on Earth, deepening our understanding of the natural world and the forces that have shaped it over the millennia.

Chapter 11: How the Grand Canyon Was Discovered

The discovery of the Grand Canyon is a tale steeped in exploration, curiosity, and the relentless human desire to uncover the unknown. The Grand Canyon, one of the most magnificent natural wonders on Earth, was unknown to European explorers for centuries, although Native American tribes had long called it home and held deep cultural and spiritual connections to the vast chasm. This discovery story is not just a single moment in history but a series of encounters, expeditions, and revelations that began thousands of years ago with indigenous peoples and culminated in its introduction to the broader world by Spanish explorers, American pioneers, and government expeditions. The story of how the Grand Canyon was discovered involves not only awe and admiration but also the struggles and dangers of traversing such a challenging and seemingly endless landscape.

Long before European explorers ever set foot in North America, the Grand Canyon was inhabited by various Native American tribes. The Ancestral Puebloans, also known as the Anasazi, were among the first known inhabitants of the region, living near the canyon's rim and within its walls over 1,200 years ago. Evidence of their existence can be found in the form of cliff dwellings, pottery, and petroglyphs scattered throughout the canyon. The Hopi, Zuni, Hualapai, Havasupai, and Navajo peoples also have deep-rooted histories in the Grand Canyon. For these tribes, the canyon was more than just a physical landmark; it was a sacred place tied to their creation stories, spiritual practices, and way of life. They viewed the canyon not as something to be "discovered" but as a place that had always been there, playing a vital role in their cultural identity and connection to the land.

For centuries, the Grand Canyon remained largely unknown to the outside world. It was hidden in plain sight, its remote location and rugged terrain making it difficult for early explorers to access. However, in 1540, during the Spanish exploration of the American Southwest, the first Europeans laid eyes on the Grand Canyon. The discovery came as part of a larger expedition led by Francisco Vásquez de Coronado, a Spanish conquistador in search of the fabled Seven Cities of Gold. Coronado's expedition, which set out from present-day Mexico, ventured into what is now the American Southwest, hoping to find vast wealth and riches. Along the way, they encountered various Native American tribes who spoke of a great chasm to the north.

Intrigued by the stories, Coronado dispatched a small scouting party led by García López de Cárdenas to investigate. In September 1540, Cárdenas and his men, guided by Hopi tribesmen, became the first Europeans to reach the South Rim of the Grand Canyon. Upon arriving at the edge, they were awestruck by the sheer size and depth of the canyon. The vast chasm stretched as far as the eye could see, and the Colorado River, which carved the canyon over millions of years, appeared as a tiny ribbon far below. However, despite their amazement, the Spanish explorers quickly realized that descending into the canyon would be nearly impossible. The steep cliffs, lack of water, and dangerous terrain made it impractical for them to explore the canyon in any meaningful way. After several attempts to find a way down to the river, Cárdenas and his men were forced to turn back, leaving the canyon largely unexplored.

For the next several centuries, the Grand Canyon remained a mystery to the outside world. Spanish missionaries and settlers passed through the region, but few ventured into the canyon itself. It wasn't until the 19th century, during the westward expansion of the United States, that the Grand Canyon began to attract the attention of American explorers and pioneers. In the early 1800s, fur trappers, prospectors, and surveyors began to move into the region in search of new opportunities, but the canyon's vast and inhospitable terrain continued to deter large-scale exploration.

One of the most significant figures in the discovery and exploration of the Grand Canyon in the 19th century was John Wesley Powell, a geologist and Civil War veteran. In 1869, Powell led the first scientific expedition to explore the Colorado River and map the canyon. Powell's expedition was no small feat, as the Colorado River was largely uncharted, and the canyon was still a forbidding and little-known landscape. The expedition consisted of ten men, four boats, and enough provisions to last for several months. The journey began in Green River, Wyoming, and the crew followed the Green and Colorado Rivers into the Grand Canyon.

The expedition faced numerous challenges, including treacherous rapids, unpredictable weather, and the loss of boats and supplies. Despite these obstacles, Powell and his men pressed on, determined to navigate the entire length of the canyon. Along the way, Powell made detailed notes about the geology, geography, and natural history of the canyon, which would later be used to create accurate maps of the region. After three months of harrowing exploration, the expedition finally emerged from the canyon, having successfully navigated the river and made the first scientific record of the Grand Canyon. Powell's expedition was a turning point in the discovery of the Grand Canyon, as it opened the door to further exploration and study of the region.

Following Powell's expedition, the Grand Canyon began to attract more attention from scientists, explorers, and tourists alike. In the late 19th and early 20th centuries, several more expeditions were launched to explore the canyon, study its geology, and map its features. The advent of the railroad in the early 1900s made the Grand Canyon more accessible to the general public, and soon it became a popular destination for tourists from around the world. The canyon's breathtaking beauty and geological significance captured the imagination of those who visited, and efforts were made to protect and preserve the area for future generations.

In 1903, President Theodore Roosevelt visited the Grand Canyon and was so moved by its grandeur that he made it a priority to protect the area as a national treasure. Roosevelt was a passionate advocate for conservation, and he recognized the importance of preserving the canyon's natural beauty and unique ecosystems. In 1908, Roosevelt designated the Grand Canyon as a national monument, and in 1919, it became a national park under the administration of the National Park Service. The designation of the Grand Canyon as a national park helped ensure its protection and opened the door to further exploration, research, and tourism.

The discovery of the Grand Canyon, however, is not just about the arrival of Europeans and Americans in the region. It is also about the long-standing relationship between Native American tribes and the canyon. For thousands of years, tribes like the Hualapai, Havasupai, Navajo, Hopi, and others have lived in and around the Grand Canyon, relying on its resources and incorporating it into their cultural and spiritual practices. The canyon is considered a sacred place by many Native American tribes, and their deep connection to the land predates the arrival of European explorers by millennia.

The Havasupai people, for example, have lived in the Grand Canyon for over 800 years, making their homes in the fertile valleys and along the canyon's rivers. They cultivated crops like corn, beans, and squash and relied on the canyon's natural resources for food, shelter, and spiritual sustenance. The Hopi, who believe the Grand Canyon is the place where their ancestors emerged into the world, have long considered the canyon to be a sacred site, central to their religious beliefs and cultural identity. Even today, Native American tribes continue to live in and around the Grand Canyon, maintaining their cultural traditions and fighting to preserve their connection to the land.

In conclusion, the discovery of the Grand Canyon is a multifaceted story that spans centuries and involves a diverse array of people, from

Native American tribes who have lived in harmony with the canyon for thousands of years to European explorers seeking new lands and American pioneers driven by curiosity and the spirit of adventure. While the canyon may have been "discovered" by Europeans in 1540 and explored more thoroughly in the 19th century, its significance to the people who have lived there for generations runs much deeper. Today, the Grand Canyon stands as one of the most iconic natural wonders in the world, a place of breathtaking beauty, geological importance, and cultural significance. Its discovery continues to inspire awe and wonder in those who visit, reminding us of the incredible power of nature and the enduring human desire to explore and understand the world around us.

Chapter 12: The Skywalk and Modern Attractions

The Skywalk and modern attractions of the Grand Canyon have significantly transformed how visitors experience this natural wonder, blending breathtaking views with innovative engineering and providing unforgettable encounters with nature. These developments mark a new chapter in the history of the Grand Canyon, as they introduce people to the canyon in ways that were previously unimaginable. The story of the Skywalk and the surrounding modern attractions begins with a vision of how to share the beauty of the Grand Canyon with the world, while still preserving its grandeur and respect for the native cultures that have long called this area home.

The Grand Canyon Skywalk is undoubtedly one of the most extraordinary man-made structures ever built at the Grand Canyon. Located on the Hualapai Indian Reservation at the canyon's western rim, the Skywalk offers visitors a unique and thrilling way to experience the vastness of the canyon by walking on a glass bridge that extends 70 feet beyond the canyon's edge. Standing 4,000 feet above the Colorado River, the Skywalk allows guests to look straight down into the canyon, giving the sensation of floating in mid-air over one of the most iconic landscapes in the world.

The idea for the Skywalk was conceived by David Jin, a Las Vegas-based entrepreneur who wanted to create a new way for people to engage with the Grand Canyon's majesty. In partnership with the Hualapai Tribe, Jin worked to design a structure that would not only provide an exhilarating experience but also respect the cultural and environmental significance of the land. The Hualapai people, whose ancestral lands encompass the western part of the Grand Canyon, were deeply involved in the planning and construction process. The tribe recognized the potential for the Skywalk to bring economic development to their community while also showcasing the natural beauty of their homeland to visitors from all over the world.

Construction on the Skywalk began in 2004 and took several years to complete. The engineering challenges were immense, as the structure needed to be able to support the weight of thousands of visitors while withstanding the forces of wind, weather, and the constant shifting of the canyon's geology. The bridge is made of specially designed glass and steel, and it can hold up to 71 million pounds of weight, which is equivalent to the weight of 71 fully loaded 747 airplanes. The materials used in the construction are incredibly strong and durable, ensuring that the Skywalk remains safe for visitors for generations to come.

The Skywalk officially opened to the public in March 2007, and it quickly became one of the Grand Canyon's most popular attractions. For many, stepping out onto the glass platform is an exhilarating and heart-pounding experience. As visitors walk out onto the bridge, the transparency of the glass gives them the sensation that they are walking on air, with nothing between them and the canyon floor far below. The views are unparalleled, offering a full 360-degree panorama of the canyon's stunning landscapes. On clear days, the visibility stretches for miles, allowing visitors to see the intricate layers of rock, the winding Colorado River, and the distant horizon, all from an entirely new perspective.

In addition to the thrill of the Skywalk itself, the surrounding area offers a range of modern attractions and amenities for visitors. Grand Canyon West, the region where the Skywalk is located, has been developed by the Hualapai Tribe as a destination that combines natural beauty with cultural education and adventure. Visitors to Grand Canyon West can enjoy a variety of activities, including helicopter tours, river rafting, zip-lining, and Native American cultural experiences. The goal of these modern attractions is to offer visitors a comprehensive experience that not only highlights the breathtaking views of the Grand Canyon but also immerses them in the history, culture, and traditions of the Hualapai people.

One of the highlights of a visit to Grand Canyon West is the opportunity to learn more about the Hualapai Tribe and their deep connection to the land. The tribe offers cultural performances, traditional storytelling, and opportunities to view and purchase authentic Native American arts and crafts. The Hualapai people have lived in the Grand Canyon region for centuries, and their history and culture are woven into the fabric of the landscape. Visitors can explore traditional dwellings, watch performances of Native dances, and learn about the tribe's spiritual beliefs, which are closely tied to the canyon and its natural features. This cultural immersion adds a rich layer of understanding to a visit to the Grand Canyon, allowing visitors to appreciate the canyon not only as a geological wonder but also as a sacred place that holds deep meaning for the people who have lived there for generations.

Beyond the Skywalk and cultural experiences, Grand Canyon West offers a range of adventure activities for thrill-seekers and nature enthusiasts. Helicopter tours are a popular option, providing visitors with the chance to see the Grand Canyon from a bird's-eye view. These tours typically take off from the canyon rim and descend into the canyon itself, offering a close-up view of the canyon's towering cliffs, hidden waterfalls, and the mighty Colorado River. Some helicopter tours also land at the bottom of the canyon, allowing visitors to explore the canyon floor and experience its rugged beauty up close. This unique perspective offers a sense of scale and grandeur that is impossible to fully grasp from the canyon rim alone.

For those looking for a more hands-on adventure, river rafting trips down the Colorado River provide an exhilarating way to experience the power and beauty of the Grand Canyon. These trips range from leisurely float tours that are suitable for families and beginners to more intense whitewater rafting expeditions for experienced adventurers.

Rafting through the Grand Canyon allows visitors to witness the canyon's towering walls from the water, see hidden waterfalls and caves, and experience the excitement of navigating the river's rapids. It's a truly immersive way to connect with the natural environment of the canyon and appreciate the forces of nature that have shaped it over millions of years.

Zip-lining is another modern attraction at Grand Canyon West that has gained popularity in recent years. The zip-line course takes visitors on a high-flying adventure over the canyon's rugged terrain, providing a thrilling ride through the air with stunning views of the canyon below. The course includes several lines of varying lengths and speeds, making it a great option for both beginners and experienced zip-liners. The rush of soaring through the air while taking in the vastness of the canyon adds an element of excitement and fun to the Grand Canyon experience.

In addition to these adventurous activities, the modern infrastructure at Grand Canyon West includes visitor centers, dining options, and accommodation facilities. The visitor center provides educational exhibits about the geology, ecology, and history of the Grand Canyon, as well as information about the Hualapai Tribe and their role in preserving and sharing this incredible landscape. Visitors can also enjoy a meal at the Skywalk Café, which offers stunning views of the canyon while serving a variety of food and drinks. For those who want to extend their stay, lodging options range from rustic cabins to more modern accommodations, allowing visitors to spend the night in this remarkable location and experience the canyon at sunrise or sunset, when the light transforms the landscape into a kaleidoscope of colors.

The development of modern attractions like the Skywalk and the amenities at Grand Canyon West has brought both opportunities and challenges. On one hand, these attractions have made the Grand Canyon more accessible to a wider audience, providing new ways for people to engage with and appreciate its beauty. They have also brought economic development to the Hualapai Tribe, creating jobs and generating revenue that supports the tribe's efforts to preserve their cultural heritage and protect the environment. On the other hand, the increased commercialization of the Grand Canyon has raised concerns about the impact of tourism on the natural landscape and the potential for cultural exploitation. Balancing the desire to share the Grand Canyon with the world while preserving its natural and cultural integrity is an ongoing challenge, one that requires careful planning and collaboration between all stakeholders.

In conclusion, the Skywalk and modern attractions at the Grand Canyon represent a fusion of adventure, culture, and natural beauty that offers visitors an unparalleled experience of one of the world's greatest natural wonders. Whether walking on the Skywalk's glass bridge, learning about the traditions of the Hualapai Tribe, or embarking on an adrenaline-filled adventure, visitors to Grand Canyon West are given the opportunity to connect with the canyon in new and exciting ways. These attractions highlight the ever-evolving relationship between people and the Grand Canyon, reminding us of the enduring power of this landscape to inspire awe and wonder, while also challenging us to think about how we can preserve and protect it for future generations to enjoy. The Skywalk is more than just a tourist attraction; it's a symbol of how innovation and respect for nature can come together to create something truly extraordinary.

Chapter 13: The Role of Weather in Shaping the Canyon

The role of weather in shaping the Grand Canyon is a critical aspect of its formation and ongoing transformation. While the Colorado River is often credited as the primary force behind the creation of the Grand Canyon, weather plays an equally significant role in its continual shaping. The interplay of water, wind, temperature fluctuations, and other weather-related processes over millions of years has carved and sculpted the canyon, giving it the dramatic features that have made it one of the most iconic landscapes in the world. From the powerful effects of erosion and weathering to the influence of seasonal changes, the impact of weather on the Grand Canyon is both subtle and immense, with every storm, flood, and gust of wind contributing to its evolution.

One of the primary ways weather shapes the Grand Canyon is through the process of erosion. Erosion is the gradual breakdown of rock and soil by natural forces such as water, wind, and ice. In the Grand Canyon, water plays the most prominent role in erosion, particularly through rainfall and runoff. When it rains, water flows down the canyon walls, carrying loose rock and sediment with it. This process of rainwater erosion is called sheet erosion, and it occurs across the surface of the canyon, slowly wearing away at the rock and deepening the canyon over time.

While the Colorado River is the most well-known water source in the Grand Canyon, rainfall is actually a more widespread and frequent contributor to erosion. The Grand Canyon experiences a monsoon season during the summer months, typically from July to September, when intense thunderstorms bring heavy rainfall to the region. These storms can produce flash floods, which occur when a large amount of rain falls in a short period of time, causing water to rush through the narrow side canyons and gullies. Flash floods are particularly powerful because the steep walls of the canyon channel the water into concentrated streams, increasing its velocity and force. As the water flows through the canyon, it picks up rocks, sand, and other debris, which act like sandpaper, grinding away at the canyon walls and deepening the canyon floor.

The effects of flash floods are most noticeable in the side canyons and tributaries that feed into the main canyon. These smaller canyons, often carved by ephemeral streams that only flow during periods of heavy rain, are shaped primarily by the sudden and violent forces of flash floods. The water flows through these narrow passageways with incredible speed, carving out new channels and reshaping the landscape in a matter of hours. Over time, repeated flash floods widen and deepen the side canyons, contributing to the overall expansion of the Grand Canyon. Some of the most famous features of the Grand Canyon, such as slot canyons and waterfalls, have been formed and sculpted by the erosive power of flash floods.

In addition to water, wind is another important factor in the weathering and erosion of the Grand Canyon. The high desert environment of the Grand Canyon is characterized by strong winds that sweep through the canyon, especially during the spring and fall. Wind erosion, also known as aeolian erosion, occurs when particles of sand and dust are carried by the wind and blasted against the canyon walls. Over time, this process wears down the rock surfaces, smoothing them and sometimes creating unique rock formations known as hoodoos, pinnacles, and arches. Wind erosion is most effective in areas where the rock is softer or more fractured, allowing the wind to chip away at the weaker material.

The canyon's layers of rock, which vary in hardness and composition, respond differently to wind erosion. For example, the softer layers of shale and sandstone are more susceptible to being worn away by wind, while the harder layers of limestone and granite resist erosion for longer periods of time. This differential erosion, where softer rock erodes faster than harder rock, is responsible for many of the dramatic cliffs, ledges, and terraces that give the Grand Canyon its distinctive topography. The wind not only erodes the rock directly but also carries away the fine particles of sand and dust that accumulate on the canyon floor, helping to keep the canyon's features exposed and visible.

Another important weather-related process that shapes the Grand Canyon is freeze-thaw weathering. This type of weathering occurs when water seeps into cracks in the rock during the day and then freezes at night. As the water freezes, it expands, exerting pressure on the surrounding rock. Over time, the repeated freezing and thawing cycle causes the cracks to widen, eventually leading to pieces of rock breaking off and falling into the canyon. This process, known as frost wedging, is particularly effective in the Grand Canyon because of the large temperature fluctuations that occur between day and night.

The Grand Canyon is located in a high desert region, where daytime temperatures can soar to over 100°F (38°C) in the summer, while nighttime temperatures can drop below freezing, especially during the winter months. These temperature swings provide the perfect conditions for freeze-thaw weathering to occur, particularly in the higher elevations of the canyon where snow and ice are more common. The rockfalls and landslides that result from frost wedging contribute to the ongoing widening of the canyon, as large sections of the canyon walls are weakened and eventually collapse. These rockfalls also add to the debris that accumulates at the base of the canyon, gradually filling in the lower sections and creating new landforms over time.

Temperature fluctuations also play a role in thermal expansion and contraction, another weather-related process that affects the Grand Canyon. Thermal expansion occurs when the rock is heated by the sun during the day, causing it to expand slightly. At night, when the temperature drops, the rock cools and contracts. This constant cycle of heating and cooling causes stress within the rock, eventually leading to fractures and the breakdown of the rock surface. While thermal expansion and contraction are slower processes compared to freeze-thaw weathering or flash floods, they still contribute to the gradual weakening and erosion of the canyon walls over long periods of time.

The role of weather in shaping the Grand Canyon extends beyond just the physical erosion of the rock. Weather also influences the biological and ecological processes that occur within the canyon, which in turn affect the landscape. For example, the types of vegetation that grow in the canyon are determined by the local climate and weather patterns. In the upper elevations of the canyon, where temperatures are cooler and precipitation is more abundant, forests of ponderosa pine and juniper trees are common. These trees help stabilize the soil and prevent erosion by their root systems, which hold the soil in place and reduce the amount of runoff during rainstorms.

In contrast, the lower elevations of the canyon, which are hotter and drier, are home to desert plants such as cacti, agave, and creosote bushes. These plants have adapted to survive in the harsh conditions of the desert, with deep root systems that allow them to access water stored deep within the ground. While these desert plants do not provide as much soil stabilization as the trees in the higher elevations, they still play a role in preventing erosion by reducing the amount of exposed soil and helping to absorb rainfall during storms. The distribution of plant life within the canyon is closely linked to the weather patterns, with different species thriving in different microclimates.

Additionally, weather patterns affect the behavior of wildlife in the Grand Canyon, which can also influence the landscape. For example, during periods of drought, animals such as deer and bighorn sheep may move to higher elevations in search of water and food, causing changes in the vegetation as they graze and trample the plants. Birds and small mammals may also seek shelter in the canyon during storms, affecting the distribution of seeds and contributing to the spread of certain plant species. The interaction between weather, plant life, and animal behavior creates a dynamic and ever-changing ecosystem that is an integral part of the Grand Canyon's landscape.

Throughout the seasons, the Grand Canyon experiences a variety of weather conditions that contribute to its ongoing transformation. In the winter, snow blankets the higher elevations of the canyon, while the lower elevations remain relatively dry. As the snow melts in the spring, it provides a source of water for the Colorado River and its tributaries, fueling the process of erosion and shaping the canyon's features. The spring also brings windy conditions, which can lead to increased wind erosion and the redistribution of sand and dust within the canyon. Summer is the hottest and most active season for weathering and erosion, as monsoon storms bring heavy rain and flash floods that carve out new channels and reshape the landscape. Finally, the cooler temperatures of fall signal the beginning of the freeze-thaw weathering process, as nighttime temperatures drop below freezing and water begins to seep into the cracks in the rock.

In conclusion, the role of weather in shaping the Grand Canyon is a complex and multifaceted process that involves the interplay of water, wind, temperature, and biological factors. Over millions of years, these weather-related processes have worked in tandem with the Colorado River to carve and sculpt the canyon's dramatic features. Erosion, weathering, and the effects of seasonal changes continue to transform the canyon, ensuring that it remains a dynamic and evolving landscape. As visitors stand on the edge of the Grand Canyon and gaze into its depths, they are witnessing the result of countless weather events, both large and small, that have shaped this natural wonder into the awe-inspiring sight it is today. Whether through the sudden force of a flash flood, the gradual breakdown of rock by frost wedging, or the gentle winds that sweep through the canyon, the weather plays an essential role in the ongoing story of the Grand Canyon's formation and evolution.

Chapter 14: The Grand Canyon's Hidden Caves and Waterfalls

The Grand Canyon, known for its immense size and breathtaking views, holds many secrets within its rugged terrain, including hidden caves and waterfalls that have fascinated explorers, scientists, and adventurers alike. These natural wonders are often overshadowed by the canyon's more prominent features, but they play a significant role in the landscape's history and ecosystem. The Grand Canyon's caves and waterfalls, though difficult to access and sometimes shrouded in mystery, offer a unique glimpse into the geological, hydrological, and ecological processes that have shaped this iconic location over millions of years. Exploring these lesser-known wonders reveals a world of intrigue and discovery, from the ancient formations of limestone caverns to the hidden waterfalls that cascade into secluded pools far below the canyon rim.

The Grand Canyon is home to over a thousand known caves, but only a small percentage of them have been explored in detail. Many of these caves are hidden deep within the canyon's towering walls, concealed by layers of rock and difficult to access due to their remote locations and rugged surroundings. Some caves are perched high on cliff faces, reachable only by skilled climbers, while others are nestled near the canyon floor, obscured by dense vegetation or rock debris. These caves, formed by millions of years of water erosion and the dissolution of limestone, provide invaluable insights into the geological history of the Grand Canyon, as well as the diverse array of flora and fauna that have inhabited the region over time.

One of the most famous caves in the Grand Canyon is the Cave of the Domes, the only cave open to the public in Grand Canyon National Park. Located on Horseshoe Mesa, this cave is an example of a limestone cavern, formed by water seeping into the rock and dissolving it over millions of years. The cave is filled with stalactites, stalagmites, and other mineral formations that provide a glimpse into the slow, gradual processes that shape the subterranean world. While the Cave of the Domes is relatively small compared to some of the massive cave systems found elsewhere in the world, it is a rare opportunity for visitors to explore one of the Grand Canyon's hidden wonders up close.

The formation of these caves is largely due to the unique geological conditions of the Grand Canyon. The canyon is composed of several layers of rock, each with different characteristics and susceptibilities to erosion. The majority of the caves are found within the Redwall Limestone layer, which was deposited around 340 million years ago during the Mississippian period when the region was covered by a shallow sea. As rainwater percolates down through the layers of rock, it becomes slightly acidic due to the presence of carbon dioxide in the atmosphere. This weakly acidic water reacts with the calcium carbonate in the limestone, slowly dissolving the rock and creating cavities and tunnels. Over time, these small voids can expand into larger cave systems, especially in areas where water flow is concentrated, such as along fault lines or fractures in the rock.

In addition to their geological significance, the Grand Canyon's caves are also important archaeological and paleontological sites. Many of the caves contain ancient artifacts left behind by the indigenous peoples who lived in the canyon thousands of years ago. These artifacts include pottery, tools, and remnants of early dwellings, providing evidence of the complex societies that once thrived in this harsh environment. Some caves also contain ancient animal bones and fossils, offering a glimpse into the prehistoric fauna that once roamed the region. For example, the remains of mammoths, ground sloths, and other Ice Age animals have been found in some of the canyon's caves, preserved by the cool, dry conditions that protect organic material from decay.

The isolation and difficult access of many caves have helped preserve their contents for thousands of years, making them valuable repositories of both natural and cultural history. For modern-day archaeologists, spelunkers, and scientists, the caves of the Grand Canyon offer a wealth of opportunities for research and discovery. However, the fragile nature of these environments means that access is often restricted to protect them from damage, ensuring that they remain intact for future generations to study and appreciate.

While the Grand Canyon's caves are hidden deep within its walls, its waterfalls are often concealed in plain sight, tucked away in remote side canyons and accessible only by arduous hikes or river trips. These waterfalls, fed by springs and seasonal runoff, are a stark contrast to the arid desert landscape that surrounds them, creating lush oases where water cascades over cliffs into crystal-clear pools. The sight and sound of waterfalls in the Grand Canyon are a welcome respite for weary travelers and offer a glimpse into the canyon's hidden hydrological system, which plays a vital role in sustaining the ecosystem.

One of the most famous waterfalls in the Grand Canyon is Havasu Falls, located on Havasu Creek, a tributary of the Colorado River. Havasu Falls is renowned for its stunning turquoise-blue water, which is colored by the high concentration of calcium carbonate and other minerals dissolved in the water. The falls drop about 100 feet into a series of pools, surrounded by vibrant greenery and towering red cliffs. Havasu Falls is located on the Havasupai Indian Reservation, and access to the falls is restricted, requiring a permit and a long hike or helicopter ride to reach the site. Despite the difficulty in reaching it, Havasu Falls is one of the most popular and iconic destinations in the Grand Canyon, attracting visitors from around the world who come to marvel at its beauty and swim in its refreshing waters.

Havasu Creek is fed by a series of natural springs, which emerge from the rock and provide a continuous source of water, even during the dry months when rainfall is scarce. These springs are part of the larger aquifer system that underlies the Grand Canyon, storing and releasing water that has filtered down through the rock layers over thousands of years. The springs not only feed waterfalls like Havasu Falls but also provide vital water sources for the plants and animals that inhabit the canyon. Without these hidden springs, life in the Grand Canyon would be much more difficult, as the arid climate and extreme temperatures make water a precious and scarce resource.

Another well-known waterfall in the Grand Canyon is Ribbon Falls, located along the North Kaibab Trail, one of the main hiking routes that descends from the North Rim to the Colorado River. Ribbon Falls is unique in that it cascades down a sheer rock face in a narrow, ribbon-like stream, creating a delicate and graceful waterfall that contrasts with the rugged terrain around it. The falls are surrounded by lush vegetation, including ferns and mosses, which thrive in the moist, shaded environment created by the waterfall. Ribbon Falls is a popular stop for hikers making the long trek to the canyon floor, offering a cool, refreshing break from the desert heat.

In addition to these more famous waterfalls, there are countless smaller, less-known waterfalls scattered throughout the Grand Canyon, hidden in remote side canyons and accessible only to the most adventurous explorers. Many of these waterfalls are seasonal, appearing only after heavy rainfall or snowmelt, when the runoff from the surrounding plateaus and cliffs funnels into the narrow canyons below. These temporary waterfalls can be just as dramatic and beautiful as their more permanent counterparts, creating a fleeting spectacle of rushing water that carves out new channels and reshapes the landscape with each storm.

The process by which waterfalls form in the Grand Canyon is closely tied to the same geological forces that created the canyon itself. As the Colorado River and its tributaries cut through the rock layers, they expose fault lines and fractures in the rock, creating natural weaknesses where water can flow. Over time, the force of the water erodes the rock, creating vertical drops where waterfalls can form. In some cases, waterfalls form where streams flow over more resistant layers of rock, creating a sharp drop as the water flows from the harder rock above to the softer rock below. In other cases, waterfalls form where underground springs emerge from the rock, creating a steady flow of water that cascades down the canyon walls.

The waterfalls of the Grand Canyon not only contribute to its stunning scenery but also play a vital role in the canyon's ecosystem. The pools and streams created by the waterfalls provide important habitats for a variety of plant and animal species, many of which are specially adapted to the unique conditions found in these environments. For example, certain species of fish, frogs, and invertebrates thrive in the cool, oxygen-rich waters of the canyon's waterfalls and streams, while desert plants and trees grow along the banks, benefiting from the moisture and shade provided by the waterfalls.

In conclusion, the hidden caves and waterfalls of the Grand Canyon are among its most fascinating and least understood features, offering a glimpse into the complex geological, hydrological, and ecological processes that have shaped this natural wonder over millions of years. From the ancient limestone caverns that tell the story of the canyon's formation to the vibrant waterfalls that provide life-sustaining water in an otherwise arid landscape, these hidden treasures add to the canyon's mystique and allure. While they may be difficult to access and explore, their beauty and significance make them an integral part of the Grand Canyon's rich tapestry of natural wonders. Whether tucked away in remote side canyons or perched high on cliff faces, the Grand Canyon's caves and waterfalls continue to captivate and inspire those who seek to uncover the secrets of this awe-inspiring landscape.

Chapter 15: The Best Hiking Trails for Families

The Grand Canyon, with its breathtaking vistas and unparalleled natural beauty, offers some of the most rewarding hiking experiences in the world. However, for families with children or those new to hiking, the sheer size and rugged terrain of the canyon can be intimidating. Fortunately, the Grand Canyon National Park also provides a variety of family-friendly hiking trails that allow visitors of all ages and experience levels to enjoy the wonders of this iconic landscape without the need for extensive gear or preparation. These trails offer a combination of scenic beauty, educational opportunities, and manageable distances that make them perfect for families seeking to explore the Grand Canyon together. From paved paths along the rim to easy descents into the canyon itself, these trails provide the chance to experience the park's unique geology, wildlife, and history while keeping safety and enjoyment at the forefront.

One of the most accessible and family-friendly hikes in the Grand Canyon is the Rim Trail, which stretches for over 13 miles along the South Rim, offering spectacular views of the canyon without the challenge of descending into its depths. The Rim Trail is mostly flat and paved, making it ideal for families with young children, strollers, or anyone who prefers an easy, leisurely walk. The trail can be accessed from numerous points along the South Rim, including popular areas like Mather Point, Yavapai Point, and the Grand Canyon Village. This flexibility allows families to tailor their hike to their abilities, whether they want to walk a short distance or spend an entire day exploring the trail.

The Rim Trail offers numerous lookout points, where families can stop and take in the panoramic views of the canyon's colorful layers, the winding Colorado River far below, and the surrounding plateaus.

Along the way, informational signs provide insights into the geology, flora, and fauna of the Grand Canyon, making the hike not only a visual treat but also an educational experience. Families can learn about the canyon's formation, its diverse ecosystems, and the role of weather in shaping the landscape. Additionally, the Rim Trail's proximity to visitor centers, restrooms, and shuttle bus stops makes it easy for families to take breaks, get snacks, and adjust their plans as needed.

For families looking for a bit more adventure without the difficulty of a steep descent, the South Kaibab Trail offers a manageable and rewarding hike. The South Kaibab Trail is known for its stunning vistas and dramatic switchbacks that lead hikers into the upper layers of the canyon. While this trail eventually descends deep into the canyon, families can enjoy a short hike to the first major landmark, Ooh Aah Point, which is just 0.9 miles from the trailhead. The hike to Ooh Aah Point is moderately challenging, with some elevation change, but it is short enough to be manageable for older children and parents in good physical condition.

Ooh Aah Point rewards hikers with one of the most breathtaking views in the Grand Canyon. From this vantage point, families can see the vast expanse of the canyon stretching out in all directions, with jagged cliffs, distant plateaus, and the winding Colorado River far below. The sense of scale is awe-inspiring, and it's a perfect spot to stop for photos, a picnic, or simply to take in the grandeur of the canyon. The hike back to the trailhead is uphill but relatively short, allowing families to experience the thrill of descending into the canyon without committing to a longer, more strenuous hike.

For families with younger children or those who prefer a more leisurely stroll, the Bright Angel Trail offers a gentler descent into the canyon. This trail, which starts near the Grand Canyon Village, is one of the most popular in the park due to its accessibility and well-maintained path. While the full trail descends all the way to the Colorado River, families can enjoy a shorter hike to one of the intermediate rest points, such as the 1.5 Mile Resthouse or the 3 Mile Resthouse. These resthouses offer shaded areas, water, and restrooms, making them ideal turnaround points for families.

The Bright Angel Trail offers a different perspective on the Grand Canyon compared to the Rim Trail. As hikers descend, they pass through the canyon's rock layers, each with its own unique color and texture. The trail is also a great place to spot wildlife, such as mule deer, squirrels, and various bird species. Families can learn about the canyon's ecosystems and the plants and animals that have adapted to survive in this harsh environment. The gradual descent of the Bright Angel Trail, combined with the availability of rest stops and the opportunity to see more of the canyon's interior, makes it a popular choice for families who want to experience the canyon beyond the rim.

Another excellent option for families is the Desert View Trail, located on the eastern end of the South Rim near the Desert View Watchtower. This easy, paved trail runs for about a mile and offers stunning views of the Colorado River, the canyon's colorful rock formations, and the surrounding desert landscape. The trail starts at the Desert View Visitor Center and follows the rim to the historic Watchtower, a stone structure designed by architect Mary Colter that offers panoramic views from its upper floors. The Desert View Trail is relatively flat and accessible, making it a great choice for families with young children or anyone looking for a short, scenic hike.

The Desert View area is less crowded than the central South Rim, providing a more peaceful and relaxed experience. Along the

trail, families can enjoy a quieter side of the Grand Canyon, with fewer visitors and more opportunities to spot wildlife like birds of prey, lizards, and other desert creatures. The views from the Desert View Watchtower are particularly striking, offering a unique perspective of the canyon and the surrounding Painted Desert. The watchtower itself is a piece of history, designed in 1932 to resemble ancient Native American structures, and families can explore its interior, where murals and artifacts provide insight into the cultural history of the region. The Desert View Trail is not only scenic but also a chance to learn about the artistic and cultural heritage of the Grand Canyon.

For those staying on the North Rim, which is higher in elevation and less visited than the South Rim, the Transept Trail is a fantastic family-friendly hike. The North Rim offers cooler temperatures and more forested surroundings, creating a different atmosphere compared to the arid South Rim. The Transept Trail is an easy 3-mile round-trip hike that follows the rim from the Grand Canyon Lodge to the North Rim Campground. Along the way, families are treated to sweeping views of the Transept Canyon, a side canyon of the Grand Canyon, as well as glimpses of the canyon's more remote and less-traveled areas.

The Transept Trail passes through lush forests of Ponderosa pines and offers plenty of opportunities for children to explore the natural surroundings. Interpretive signs along the trail provide information about the geology and ecology of the North Rim, making the hike educational as well as scenic. Families can take their time along this relatively short trail, stopping at benches and lookout points to enjoy the serene beauty of the North Rim. The Transept Trail is a great introduction to the North Rim's hiking options, which tend to be less strenuous and more peaceful due to the smaller number of visitors.

For a more immersive experience in the canyon's ecosystems, the Grandview Trail offers families the opportunity to explore the upper reaches of the canyon without the need for an extended hike. The Grandview Trailhead is located about 12 miles east of Grand Canyon Village, and while the full trail is considered strenuous, families can hike just a short distance along the upper section to experience the canyon's beauty and solitude. The trail descends steeply at first, but families can turn around at any point, allowing for a flexible and customizable hike.

The upper portion of the Grandview Trail offers some of the most spectacular views of the Grand Canyon, with fewer crowds and more opportunities for solitude. This trail is also known for its rich history, as it was originally built in the late 1800s by miners seeking copper in the canyon. Families can learn about the area's mining history and imagine what it was like for early explorers and miners to navigate this rugged terrain. While the descent can be challenging, hiking just the first section provides a sense of adventure without the need for an all-day hike.

For those seeking a truly unique and memorable experience, the Grand Canyon also offers ranger-led family programs and educational hikes that cater to younger visitors. These guided hikes, often held during the summer months, provide families with the chance to explore the park with a knowledgeable ranger who can point out interesting features, answer questions, and share stories about the Grand Canyon's history, geology, and wildlife. Ranger-led programs are typically designed to be accessible and engaging for children, making them a great way for families to connect with the park's natural wonders in a fun and interactive way.

In addition to hiking, families visiting the Grand Canyon can take advantage of other family-friendly activities, such as visiting the Grand Canyon Visitor Center, where interactive exhibits and films provide an in-depth look at the park's geology and history. The Junior Ranger Program, available at both the South and North Rims, is another fantastic opportunity for children to learn about the Grand Canyon while earning a badge by completing educational activities. Families can also enjoy scenic drives along the rim, stopping at various viewpoints for picnics and photo opportunities.

Safety is a top priority when hiking with families in the Grand Canyon, and it's important to be prepared for the unique challenges of hiking in the desert. The weather can be hot and dry, especially during the summer months, so families should carry plenty of water, wear sunscreen, and take breaks in the shade to avoid heat exhaustion. It's also important to stay on designated trails and avoid venturing too close to the edge of the canyon, as the terrain can be steep and unstable in some areas. Families should start their hikes early in the morning or later in the afternoon to avoid the midday heat and always check the weather forecast before setting out.

In conclusion, the Grand Canyon offers a variety of hiking trails that are perfect for families, from easy rim walks to more adventurous descents into the canyon. Whether exploring the paved Rim Trail, hiking to Ooh Aah Point on the South Kaibab Trail, or discovering the quiet beauty of the North Rim on the Transept Trail, families can enjoy the park's stunning scenery and learn about its natural and cultural history along the way. With proper preparation and a sense of adventure, a family hike in the Grand Canyon can be a memorable and rewarding experience that creates lasting memories for visitors of all ages.

Chapter 16: Stargazing at the Grand Canyon

Stargazing at the Grand Canyon is an experience unlike any other. With its vast, dark skies, far removed from the light pollution of cities, the Grand Canyon offers one of the best places on Earth to observe the cosmos. For families, astronomers, and anyone with an appreciation for the night sky, the Grand Canyon transforms after sunset into a celestial wonderland. The clear desert air and high elevation, especially along the South and North Rims, make the canyon an ideal destination for stargazers. The grandeur of the Grand Canyon's geological formations, coupled with the awe-inspiring beauty of the night sky, creates a breathtaking setting for stargazing that draws visitors from around the world.

The Grand Canyon National Park has made a concerted effort to preserve its dark skies and reduce light pollution, earning it recognition as an International Dark Sky Park. This status means that the park is committed to protecting the natural night environment, ensuring that future generations can experience the same wonder of stargazing that visitors enjoy today. With minimal artificial lighting and vast open spaces, the Grand Canyon offers an unparalleled opportunity to observe stars, planets, and deep-sky objects such as galaxies and nebulae. On clear nights, stargazers can witness the Milky Way in all its splendor, stretching across the sky like a shimmering river of light.

One of the most popular spots for stargazing in the Grand Canyon is the South Rim, particularly at locations like Mather Point, Yavapai Point, and Desert View. These viewpoints not only provide expansive views of the canyon itself but also serve as excellent locations for gazing up at the stars. Mather Point, located near the Grand Canyon Visitor Center, is a favorite for stargazers because it's easily accessible and offers wide, open skies. Here, the horizon seems to melt into the sky, giving stargazers the feeling of being on the edge of the world as they look out into the vast universe. Desert View, on the eastern end of the South Rim, is another excellent stargazing location, with its historic Watchtower serving as a unique backdrop to the nighttime spectacle.

For families and beginner stargazers, the Grand Canyon National Park often hosts organized stargazing events and astronomy programs led by park rangers and professional astronomers. These programs are held during the summer months when the weather is warm and the skies are consistently clear. One of the highlights is the annual Grand Canyon Star Party, which takes place over eight nights in June. During this event, amateur astronomers from across the country set up their telescopes at the South and North Rims, offering visitors the chance to look through high-powered equipment and view celestial objects up close. Volunteers are available to answer questions, share their knowledge, and guide visitors through the constellations, planets, and other phenomena visible in the night sky.

The Grand Canyon Star Party is a magical experience for stargazers of all ages. On any given night during the event, hundreds of people gather at designated viewing areas to enjoy the spectacle of the night sky. Telescopes are aimed at distant galaxies, Saturn's rings, the moons of Jupiter, or deep-sky nebulae, while astronomers provide commentary and explain the science behind what visitors are seeing. Children and adults alike are often amazed by their first glimpses of planets or stars that are millions of light-years away. The event also features nightly presentations on astronomy and the importance of preserving dark skies, making it both educational and entertaining for the whole family.

For those who prefer a more solitary or peaceful stargazing experience, the North Rim of the Grand Canyon offers an alternative to the busier South Rim. With fewer visitors and a more remote location, the North Rim provides a quieter and more intimate setting for stargazing. The North Rim is higher in elevation than the South

Rim, which can result in clearer, crisper skies, particularly during the summer months. Visitors can find secluded spots along the rim, such as at Bright Angel Point or Cape Royal, where they can set up blankets, telescopes, or simply lie back and gaze at the stars. The North Rim's relative isolation and lack of light pollution make it an ideal place to experience the full brilliance of the night sky.

As the sun sets over the Grand Canyon, the transition from daylight to darkness is a spectacle in itself. Watching the sky turn from a golden orange to deep purples and blues, as the canyon's cliffs and plateaus become silhouetted against the fading light, is a mesmerizing experience. Once the last traces of sunlight disappear, the stars begin to emerge, first one by one and then in an ever-increasing cascade. On moonless nights, the sky becomes a vast canvas of stars, with the Milky Way arching across the sky like a cosmic highway. Even without telescopes, the naked eye is sufficient to observe a multitude of stars, constellations, and meteors.

The Grand Canyon's position at a relatively low latitude in the Northern Hemisphere provides a unique view of both northern and southern celestial objects. Depending on the time of year, stargazers can see constellations such as Orion, Ursa Major, and Cassiopeia in the northern sky, as well as Sagittarius, Scorpius, and Centaurus in the southern sky. During the summer months, the bright star Vega dominates the night sky, while in the winter, the constellation Orion becomes a prominent feature. The clarity of the Grand Canyon's dark skies also makes it possible to see fainter celestial objects that are often invisible in more light-polluted areas, such as star clusters, faint nebulae, and distant galaxies.

For families interested in learning more about the constellations, the Grand Canyon National Park offers a variety of resources, including star maps and apps that help visitors identify stars and planets in real-time. Many visitors find it exciting to learn the stories behind the constellations, tracing the outlines of mythological figures like Orion the Hunter, Hercules, and the winged horse Pegasus. Stargazing at the Grand Canyon not only provides a visual feast but also allows for a deeper connection to the history and mythology of the stars, as well as the scientific wonder of the universe.

In addition to its role as a stargazing destination, the Grand Canyon plays a significant part in ongoing astronomical research. The park's dark skies provide an ideal environment for scientists studying celestial phenomena, and visitors may even have the opportunity to participate in citizen science programs related to astronomy. By tracking and reporting meteor showers, changes in star brightness, or other celestial events, visitors can contribute to scientific discoveries while enjoying their time under the stars.

Another unique feature of stargazing at the Grand Canyon is the opportunity to observe natural light shows, such as meteor showers or lunar eclipses. The canyon's dark skies offer some of the best views of annual meteor showers, including the Perseids in August and the Geminids in December. During these events, stargazers can see dozens of meteors streak across the sky every hour, creating a magical and awe-inspiring display. On clear nights with a full moon, the canyon itself takes on an ethereal glow, with the cliffs and plateaus illuminated by moonlight, adding to the otherworldly atmosphere.

For visitors seeking to capture the beauty of the night sky, the Grand Canyon is also a prime location for astrophotography. The clear, dark skies provide ideal conditions for photographing the Milky Way, star trails, and other celestial phenomena. Photographers can capture stunning images of the stars with the canyon's jagged cliffs and rock formations in the foreground, creating a dramatic and visually striking contrast between Earth and sky. Many amateur photographers find the Grand Canyon's night sky to be one of the most rewarding subjects to capture, whether they are using a smartphone or a professional-grade camera.

Stargazing at the Grand Canyon is more than just an opportunity to look at the stars – it's an experience that fosters a sense of wonder, curiosity, and connection to the universe. The sheer scale of the night sky, combined with the majesty of the canyon itself, can be a humbling reminder of our place in the cosmos. For many visitors, stargazing at the Grand Canyon becomes a transformative experience, inspiring a lifelong interest in astronomy and a deeper appreciation for the natural world. Whether attending the Grand Canyon Star Party, joining a ranger-led night hike, or simply lying under the stars with family, stargazing at the Grand Canyon is a magical and unforgettable adventure.

Chapter 17: Protecting the Grand Canyon for the Future

Protecting the Grand Canyon for future generations is one of the most important and complex conservation efforts in the United States. This natural wonder, a UNESCO World Heritage Site and one of the Seven Natural Wonders of the World, faces numerous challenges that require diligent stewardship and comprehensive protection strategies. The Grand Canyon, with its immense geological, ecological, and cultural significance, represents not just a stunning natural landscape but also a symbol of the importance of preserving our planet's most precious places. As millions of visitors come to the Grand Canyon each year, the balance between human interaction and environmental preservation becomes increasingly critical. Safeguarding this iconic landmark for future generations involves addressing issues such as environmental degradation, climate change, human impact, water usage, and the preservation of cultural heritage.

One of the most pressing threats to the Grand Canyon's future is environmental degradation caused by overuse, development, and pollution. Each year, over six million people visit the Grand Canyon National Park, drawn by its breathtaking views and vast natural beauty. While tourism is vital to the local economy and offers countless people the opportunity to experience the canyon's wonders, the sheer volume of visitors also strains the park's infrastructure and natural resources. Increased foot traffic along trails can cause soil erosion, damage to vegetation, and disruption of wildlife habitats. Littering, pollution from vehicles, and light pollution from nearby developments further threaten the pristine nature of the park. The challenge for conservationists is to ensure that the Grand Canyon remains accessible and enjoyable for visitors while minimizing its ecological footprint. This delicate balancing act involves ongoing efforts to regulate visitor behavior, enhance sustainable tourism practices, and invest in infrastructure that minimizes environmental harm.

Efforts to mitigate human impact include education campaigns designed to encourage responsible behavior among visitors. The "Leave No Trace" principles are a cornerstone of these educational initiatives, teaching visitors to respect the environment by packing out all trash, staying on designated trails, and avoiding disturbance of wildlife. Additionally, the park has implemented regulations to reduce vehicle emissions and limit congestion, such as promoting shuttle systems that reduce the number of personal vehicles driving through the park. By offering alternative transportation options, the park reduces pollution and wear on roads while providing visitors with a more eco-friendly way to experience the Grand Canyon.

Another critical aspect of protecting the Grand Canyon for the future is the management of water resources. The mighty Colorado River, which carved the Grand Canyon over millions of years, is also a vital source of water for millions of people in the southwestern United States. The river's flow is controlled by a series of dams, most notably the Glen Canyon Dam, which creates Lake Powell upstream from the Grand Canyon. While these dams provide water and hydroelectric power to the region, they also have significant ecological impacts on the river and the canyon itself. The altered flow of the Colorado River has disrupted the natural sediment deposition processes, leading to changes in the canyon's ecosystem, such as the loss of sandbars and the decline of native fish species. Restoring the natural flow of the river and finding sustainable ways to manage water usage are essential to preserving the Grand Canyon's ecological integrity.

In recent years, there have been ongoing debates about the future of the Glen Canyon Dam and whether measures such as periodic "high-flow" releases should be continued to mimic the natural flood cycles that once shaped the canyon's landscape. These controlled floods help rebuild sandbars and restore habitats for native species, but they must be carefully managed to avoid negative downstream impacts. The issue of water conservation is further complicated by the increasing demand for water in the arid southwestern United States. With climate change exacerbating drought conditions and reducing water availability, balancing human water needs with the health of the Colorado River and the Grand Canyon ecosystem will be a significant challenge in the years to come.

Climate change is another existential threat to the future of the Grand Canyon. Rising global temperatures, prolonged droughts, and changing precipitation patterns are already having a noticeable impact on the canyon's environment. Warmer temperatures are altering the timing and intensity of seasonal weather patterns, affecting everything from the flow of the Colorado River to the types of plant and animal species that can survive in the region. For example, drought conditions have led to reduced vegetation, making it harder for wildlife to find food and shelter. As the climate continues to change, certain species may be forced to migrate to higher elevations or cooler areas, disrupting the balance of the ecosystem. The iconic ponderosa pines and other native species may struggle to survive if temperatures continue to rise, and invasive species that thrive in warmer conditions could further destabilize the region's biodiversity.

Park officials and conservationists are working to develop strategies to adapt to these changing conditions. One approach is to enhance habitat restoration efforts, ensuring that native plants and animals have the resources they need to thrive even as the environment changes. Conservationists are also exploring ways to create climate-resilient ecosystems by planting drought-resistant vegetation and managing water resources more efficiently. Research and monitoring programs are critical to understanding the long-term impacts of climate change on the Grand Canyon and devising solutions to mitigate those effects.

In addition to environmental concerns, protecting the Grand Canyon for future generations also involves preserving the cultural and historical significance of the area. The Grand Canyon has been home to Native American tribes for thousands of years, and it holds deep spiritual and cultural meaning for these communities. Today, several tribes, including the Havasupai, Hopi, Navajo, Hualapai, and Zuni, continue to maintain strong cultural ties to the canyon. Protecting the cultural heritage of the Grand Canyon means ensuring that these tribes have a voice in the management and preservation of the land. Efforts to collaborate with tribal communities include respecting their sacred sites, promoting the inclusion of indigenous knowledge in conservation practices, and supporting tribal initiatives to manage and protect their ancestral lands.

The federal government and conservation organizations have made strides in recent years to involve Native American tribes in decisions related to the Grand Canyon's protection. In 2016, the establishment of the Bears Ears National Monument in nearby Utah was a significant victory for tribal sovereignty, though subsequent political debates have continued to impact the scope of protections in the region. Many Native American communities are advocating for the creation of a new Grand Canyon Tribal National Park, which would give them greater authority over the management and preservation of the lands surrounding the canyon. Such initiatives reflect the importance of protecting not only the physical environment of the Grand Canyon but also the cultural legacy that is intertwined with its history.

Mining and resource extraction pose another significant threat to the future of the Grand Canyon. Uranium mining, in particular, has been a contentious issue, with concerns about the environmental and health risks associated with mining operations near the canyon. The potential for contamination of groundwater and the Colorado River has raised alarms among conservationists, Native American tribes, and public health advocates. In response to these concerns, the federal government placed a temporary moratorium on new uranium mining claims in the Grand Canyon watershed in 2012, but the debate over whether to extend or make this ban permanent continues. Protecting the Grand Canyon from harmful resource extraction is crucial to ensuring that future generations can enjoy its beauty and that its ecosystems remain intact.

Public awareness and advocacy are essential components of efforts to protect the Grand Canyon. Numerous environmental organizations, such as the Grand Canyon Trust, the Sierra Club, and the National Parks Conservation Association, work tirelessly to raise awareness about the threats facing the canyon and advocate for policies that protect its future. These groups engage in public education campaigns, legal advocacy, and grassroots organizing to ensure that the Grand Canyon remains a priority for policymakers and the public. Through their efforts, they have successfully fought off proposals for new mining operations, advocated for stronger environmental protections, and secured funding for conservation projects.

At the same time, individual visitors to the Grand Canyon can play a crucial role in its preservation. By practicing responsible tourism, following park guidelines, and supporting conservation efforts, visitors can help reduce the environmental impact of their visit and contribute to the protection of this natural wonder. Programs like the Grand Canyon Association offer visitors the chance to become involved in volunteer opportunities, from trail maintenance to habitat restoration, giving them a hands-on way to make a positive difference.

The future of the Grand Canyon depends on a combination of local, national, and global efforts to address the various environmental, cultural, and economic challenges it faces. As climate change accelerates and human demands on natural resources continue to grow, the need for comprehensive and forward-thinking conservation strategies has never been more urgent. By protecting the Grand Canyon today, we ensure that future generations will be able to experience its grandeur, learn from its history, and find inspiration in its timeless beauty. Preserving the Grand Canyon is not just about maintaining a tourist destination; it is about safeguarding one of the most extraordinary natural wonders of the world and all that it represents for humanity and the planet.

Chapter 18: How to Stay Safe While Exploring the Canyon

Staying safe while exploring the Grand Canyon is essential, as this immense and rugged landscape, while breathtakingly beautiful, can also present numerous hazards. The canyon's steep cliffs, unpredictable weather, remote trails, and wild animals make safety precautions a necessity for all visitors. With the right preparation, knowledge, and respect for the environment, exploring the Grand Canyon can be an enjoyable and awe-inspiring experience without putting yourself at unnecessary risk. Whether you are hiking the trails, riding a mule, rafting the Colorado River, or simply standing at the canyon's rim, it's important to understand the potential dangers and how to mitigate them to ensure a safe visit.

One of the most important safety considerations at the Grand Canyon is the terrain itself. The canyon is known for its dramatic drops and sharp elevation changes, and staying on designated trails and paths is crucial to avoiding accidents. It's tempting to wander off for a closer look at the views or to find a more secluded spot, but the edges of the canyon can be unstable, and loose rock or gravel can cause slips and falls. Visitors should resist the urge to climb over barriers or approach the edge for photos, as a misstep near the rim can result in a fatal fall. Hundreds of rescue missions occur each year because of hikers or sightseers who overestimate their abilities or underestimate the hazards of the terrain. For this reason, respecting all warning signs and staying within marked boundaries is critical to staying safe.

Hiking in the Grand Canyon is a popular activity, but it requires careful planning and preparation due to the challenging environment. Even short hikes can become dangerous if you're not adequately prepared. One of the most significant risks for hikers is dehydration. The Grand Canyon's desert climate can lead to extreme heat, especially in the summer months, where temperatures on the canyon floor can exceed 100 degrees Fahrenheit. Many visitors aren't accustomed to these conditions and may underestimate how much water they need. It's recommended that hikers carry plenty of water—at least one gallon per person per day—along with electrolyte-replenishing drinks to avoid dehydration. Without proper hydration, hikers are at risk for heat exhaustion or heat stroke, which can be life-threatening.

Another common mistake hikers make is underestimating the physical challenge of hiking in the canyon. Most hikes begin with a descent into the canyon, which may feel easy at first. However, what goes down must come up, and the climb back out of the canyon can be physically taxing, especially in the heat. Many visitors overestimate their ability to hike back up, leading to exhaustion and the need for emergency assistance. It's crucial to pace yourself, know your limits, and plan your hike according to your fitness level. The National Park Service encourages hikers to "hike smart," which means turning around before you feel too tired, as the ascent will require significantly more energy.

Visitors should also be aware of the wildlife that calls the Grand Canyon home. While the animals in the park are generally not aggressive, it's important to remember that they are wild, and their behavior can be unpredictable. The Grand Canyon is home to animals such as mule deer, bighorn sheep, coyotes, and various reptiles, including venomous rattlesnakes. When hiking or exploring the park, it's important to give all wildlife plenty of space. Keep your distance, never feed animals, and avoid approaching them, as they may feel threatened and react defensively. If you encounter a snake, remain calm and back away slowly. Snakes are more likely to strike if they feel cornered or surprised, so giving them a wide berth is essential.

Another safety concern for visitors is the weather, which can change rapidly in the Grand Canyon. While the park is known for its hot, dry conditions, temperatures can fluctuate significantly, especially between the rim and the canyon floor. In the winter, snow and ice can make trails slippery and dangerous, particularly on the North Rim, which sits at a higher elevation. Thunderstorms are common in the summer months, and lightning poses a serious danger, particularly to those standing on exposed ridges or near metal objects. During a thunderstorm, the safest course of action is to seek shelter in a building or vehicle. If you're caught outdoors, avoid open spaces, ridgelines, and tall objects like trees, which can attract lightning strikes.

In addition to heat, cold, and storms, flash floods are another weather-related danger in the Grand Canyon. Sudden, heavy rains can cause water levels to rise rapidly in the Colorado River and its tributaries, leading to dangerous flooding conditions. Flash floods can occur even if it isn't raining where you are, as storms upstream can send surges of water downstream. If you are hiking in a slot canyon or along a creek, it's important to be aware of the potential for flash floods and move to higher ground if you see signs of rising water. Checking the weather forecast and being aware of flood warnings before heading out on a hike can help you avoid dangerous situations.

When exploring the canyon, it's also important to carry the right gear. Proper footwear is essential, as the trails can be rocky, uneven, and slippery, especially after rain or snow. Sturdy, well-fitting hiking boots with good ankle support are recommended to reduce the risk of injury. Wearing layered clothing is also advised, as temperatures can change throughout the day. A lightweight, long-sleeved shirt can protect you from the sun during hot days, while a warm jacket will be necessary for cooler evenings or higher elevations. Sun protection is critical as well, as the canyon's high elevation and exposed landscape mean that UV radiation can be intense. Wearing sunscreen, a hat, and sunglasses will help protect your skin and eyes from sunburn and heat-related illness.

For those planning to camp overnight in the Grand Canyon, additional safety precautions should be taken. Backcountry camping requires a permit, and it's important to familiarize yourself with the park's regulations to ensure a safe experience. Campers should be prepared for cold nighttime temperatures, even in summer, and bring appropriate gear, such as a warm sleeping bag and a tent. Food storage is also crucial to avoid attracting wildlife, particularly animals like raccoons and squirrels, which can cause damage to tents and gear in search of food. In some areas, bears may also be present, and campers must use bear-proof food containers to prevent encounters with these animals.

One of the most essential safety measures when exploring the Grand Canyon is letting someone know your plans. Whether you're hiking, camping, or embarking on a rafting trip, always inform a friend, family member, or park ranger of your itinerary. Cell phone service is limited in many areas of the park, especially within the canyon itself, so it's important to have a communication plan in place in case of an emergency. Carrying a map, compass, or GPS device is also recommended, as trails can be difficult to navigate, and it's easy to become disoriented in the vast expanse of the canyon. In addition, packing a first aid kit and knowing basic first aid techniques can be lifesaving in the event of an injury or medical emergency.

For those planning more adventurous activities, such as rafting the Colorado River, additional safety measures are necessary. White-water rafting can be exhilarating, but the river's rapids can be extremely challenging, especially for beginners. It's important to book trips through reputable rafting companies that provide experienced guides and proper safety equipment. Wearing a life jacket at all times is mandatory, and following the guide's instructions is essential for staying safe on the river. The water in the Colorado River is also very cold, even during the summer months, so being prepared for immersion and knowing how to stay warm if you fall into the water is crucial.

If you're planning a trip to the Grand Canyon, it's also important to educate yourself about altitude sickness. The South Rim of the Grand

Canyon sits at an elevation of about 7,000 feet above sea level, while the North Rim is even higher, at over 8,000 feet. For visitors who are not accustomed to high altitudes, the change in elevation can cause symptoms such as headaches, dizziness, nausea, and shortness of breath. To prevent altitude sickness, it's important to stay hydrated, avoid overexertion, and allow your body time to acclimate to the higher elevation. If symptoms become severe, descending to a lower elevation and resting are the best remedies.

Staying safe in the Grand Canyon requires preparation, awareness, and respect for the natural environment. By following safety guidelines, carrying the right gear, and being mindful of potential hazards, visitors can enjoy the beauty of the canyon while minimizing the risks. Whether you're hiking, camping, rafting, or simply taking in the views from the rim, understanding the challenges and taking the necessary precautions will help ensure a memorable and safe adventure in one of the world's most awe-inspiring natural landscapes. The Grand Canyon is a place of wonder and adventure, but it's also a place where safety must always come first.

Chapter 19: The Legends and Myths of the Grand Canyon

The Grand Canyon, with its vast, awe-inspiring landscapes, towering rock formations, and mysterious depths, has long been a place of wonder and reverence. Over the centuries, this natural wonder has inspired countless legends and myths, many of which reflect the canyon's grandeur, its dangerous beauty, and the ancient peoples who once lived within its shadow. These stories, passed down through generations, blend historical fact, spiritual beliefs, and imaginative lore, creating a tapestry of myths that continue to captivate visitors and scholars alike. From the tales of Native American tribes to modern-day folklore, the Grand Canyon's legends add layers of meaning to the experience of this immense and ancient place, weaving together themes of creation, transformation, mystery, and magic.

One of the most enduring sources of myth surrounding the Grand Canyon comes from the Native American tribes who have lived in and around the area for thousands of years. For these indigenous people, the Grand Canyon is not merely a geological formation but a sacred place, deeply embedded in their cultural and spiritual beliefs. Among the most prominent of these tribes is the Hopi, whose ancestors are believed to have inhabited the canyon's cliffs and caves long ago. The Hopi people view the Grand Canyon as a portal between the present world and the underworld, a mystical realm where their ancestors emerged at the beginning of time. According to Hopi legend, the world we live in today is the Fourth World, and the canyon is the place where their ancestors climbed up from the Third World to begin a new existence. The Hopi believe that after the destruction of each previous world, their people were guided through the Grand Canyon by a deity known as Maasaw, who helped them reach safety in the higher worlds. These myths, rich in symbolism and meaning, emphasize the canyon as a place of both endings and beginnings, where the natural and supernatural worlds intersect.

The Havasupai, a Native American tribe that has lived within the Grand Canyon for over 800 years, also have deep spiritual connections to the land and its legends. Known as the "People of the Blue-Green Waters," the Havasupai have a rich oral tradition that includes stories about the formation of the canyon and the surrounding area. One of their most famous myths tells the story of the creation of Havasu Falls, a breathtaking waterfall located within Havasu Canyon, a tributary of the Grand Canyon. According to legend, the Havasupai's ancestors were in great need of water during a time of drought. A young maiden from the tribe prayed to the gods for help, and her prayers were answered when a spring miraculously burst from the ground, eventually forming the beautiful blue-green pools and cascading falls that are still revered by the Havasupai today. This myth underscores the tribe's deep connection to the land and the life-sustaining water that flows through the canyon, and it reflects the importance of balance and respect for nature in their culture.

The Navajo, another major tribe in the region, also have their own myths associated with the Grand Canyon. In Navajo tradition, the canyon is believed to be the result of the actions of the Holy People, supernatural beings who shaped the world. One of the most prominent figures in Navajo mythology is Changing Woman, a deity associated with the cycles of life and nature. According to Navajo legend, Changing Woman created the four sacred mountains that mark the boundaries of the Navajo homeland, and the Grand Canyon is said to be part of this sacred landscape. The Navajo also believe that the spirits of their ancestors dwell within the canyon, making it a place of deep spiritual significance. The towering cliffs, expansive vistas, and mysterious caves of the Grand Canyon are seen as manifestations of the Holy People's power, and the canyon itself is viewed as a living entity that must be treated with respect and reverence.

Beyond the stories of the Native American tribes, the Grand Canyon has also inspired a wealth of legends and myths in more recent history. One of the most intriguing modern legends surrounding the canyon is the story of a mysterious underground city, often referred to as the Lost City of the Grand Canyon. In 1909, a newspaper article published in the Arizona Gazette claimed that an explorer named G.E. Kinkaid had discovered an ancient underground city within a cave in the Grand Canyon. According to the article, the city was filled with artifacts that resembled those of ancient Egypt, including statues, hieroglyphs, and golden treasures. Kinkaid allegedly reported that the cave system extended deep into the canyon, with tunnels leading to various chambers filled with relics from a forgotten civilization. Despite the sensational nature of the story, no evidence of such a city has ever been found, and the tale is widely regarded as a hoax. Nevertheless, the legend of the Lost City continues to capture the imagination of those who visit the Grand Canyon, sparking speculation about the hidden secrets that might lie beneath the canyon's surface.

Another modern legend linked to the Grand Canyon is the story of the "Canyon Dwellers," a mysterious group of people who are said to live in the remote and inaccessible areas of the canyon. According to some versions of the legend, these people are descendants of ancient civilizations who retreated into the canyon to escape persecution or natural disasters. Others suggest that they are a reclusive group of hermits or survivalists who have chosen to live off the grid, far from the reaches of modern society. While there is little evidence to support the existence of such a group, the rugged and remote nature of the canyon lends itself to speculation, and the idea of a hidden community living in the depths of the canyon continues to fuel the imagination of adventurers and conspiracy theorists alike.

In addition to these tales, the Grand Canyon is also home to numerous ghost stories and supernatural legends. One of the most famous ghost stories associated with the canyon is the tale of the "Wailing Woman," a spectral figure who is said to haunt the North Rim. According to legend, the Wailing Woman is the ghost of a mother who lost her child in a tragic accident at the canyon. Heartbroken and consumed by grief, she is said to have wandered the rim in search of her lost child until she ultimately fell to her death. Visitors to the North Rim have reported hearing the eerie sounds of a woman sobbing or wailing late at night, and some claim to have seen a ghostly figure dressed in white near the edge of the canyon. While skeptics attribute these sightings and sounds to the wind or natural echoes in the canyon, the legend of the Wailing Woman continues to persist, adding a sense of mystery and melancholy to the already haunting beauty of the Grand Canyon.

The legends and myths of the Grand Canyon are as varied and complex as the landscape itself. Whether rooted in ancient Native American traditions, modern-day conspiracy theories, or ghostly folklore, these stories reflect the deep sense of awe and wonder that the canyon inspires. They remind us that the Grand Canyon is more than just a geological formation—it is a place of mystery, transformation, and spiritual significance. For the Native American tribes who have called the canyon home for thousands of years, it is a sacred place where the physical and spiritual worlds are intertwined, a portal between past and present, life and death. For modern visitors, the canyon's myths and legends add an extra layer of intrigue to the experience of exploring its vast and rugged terrain, inviting us to ponder the hidden histories and untold stories that lie beneath the surface of this natural wonder.

As we continue to explore and study the Grand Canyon, new discoveries and interpretations of its legends are sure to emerge. Whether it's the tale of an ancient underground city, the mysterious wail of a ghostly woman, or the deep spiritual beliefs of the Hopi and Navajo, the myths of the Grand Canyon will continue to captivate and inspire those who visit this magnificent place. These stories, passed down through generations, serve as a reminder of the canyon's enduring power and its place in the human imagination. They teach us to respect the natural world, to seek out the unknown, and to remember that even in a place as well-explored as the Grand Canyon, there is always room for mystery and wonder.

Chapter 20: The Grand Canyon's Place in American History

The Grand Canyon holds a prominent place in American history, both as a natural wonder and as a symbol of the vast, untamed beauty of the United States. Its history is deeply intertwined with the story of the American frontier, Native American cultures, scientific discovery, environmental conservation, and the development of the National Park system. Over millions of years, the Grand Canyon was shaped by geological forces, but it is its place in human history, particularly within the American imagination, that gives it its unique cultural significance. From the earliest Native American inhabitants who revered the canyon as a sacred site, to the explorers, scientists, and pioneers who sought to chart its depths, to its designation as one of the nation's most iconic natural landmarks, the Grand Canyon represents not just a remarkable geographical feature, but also a symbol of exploration, perseverance, and the enduring need to preserve the natural wonders of the world.

Long before European settlers arrived in North America, the Grand Canyon was home to Native American tribes, many of whom viewed it as a place of profound spiritual importance. For thousands of years, these indigenous peoples lived in and around the canyon, drawing sustenance from its resources and embedding it into their cultural and religious practices. The Ancestral Puebloans, one of the earliest known groups to inhabit the canyon, left behind evidence of their presence in the form of cliff dwellings and artifacts, some of which date back as far as 12,000 years. Their descendants, such as the Hopi, Havasupai, Navajo, and Zuni, continued to live in the region, each with their own beliefs and stories tied to the canyon's formation and its place in the world. For the Hopi, the canyon was considered the place where their ancestors emerged into the present world, while the Havasupai, whose name means "people of the blue-green water," lived in the canyon and revered its waterfalls and lush plant life. The canyon's role as a spiritual and cultural center for these tribes highlights its significance not just as a natural landmark, but as a living part of their heritage.

The first Europeans to lay eyes on the Grand Canyon were Spanish explorers in the mid-16th century, during an expedition led by García López de Cárdenas in 1540. Cárdenas and his men, who were part of Francisco Vázquez de Coronado's larger expedition in search of the mythical Seven Cities of Gold, were guided by local Native Americans to the canyon's edge. They were astonished by the sheer scale of the canyon, but despite their best efforts, they were unable to descend into its depths due to the steep cliffs and lack of water. This initial European encounter with the canyon was brief and did not result in any significant exploration or settlement, as the Spanish were more focused on their quest for gold. For the next few centuries, the canyon remained largely unknown to the outside world, a mysterious and inaccessible feature in the remote desert of the American Southwest.

It wasn't until the mid-19th century, during the period of westward expansion in the United States, that the Grand Canyon began to attract significant attention from explorers, geologists, and the American government. In 1869, a one-armed Civil War veteran and geologist named John Wesley Powell led the first documented expedition down the Colorado River through the Grand Canyon. Powell's journey was both dangerous and groundbreaking; he and his crew navigated treacherous rapids in wooden boats, often portaging around the most hazardous sections of the river. Powell's expedition provided the first detailed maps and scientific descriptions of the canyon, and his accounts of the journey captured the public's imagination, painting a picture of the canyon as a place of both peril and beauty. Powell's exploration was instrumental in advancing geological knowledge of the region, and he became a prominent advocate for the preservation of the canyon and its surrounding areas.

His efforts laid the groundwork for future conservation initiatives and helped to solidify the Grand Canyon's place in the scientific and cultural landscape of the United States.

As more explorers, scientists, and settlers ventured into the Grand Canyon, its significance in American history grew. By the late 19th century, the canyon had become a popular destination for adventure-seekers and tourists, drawn by its breathtaking vistas and the sense of awe it inspired. At the same time, commercial interests began to recognize the potential of the canyon as a site for development, with proposals for mining, dam-building, and railroads threatening to alter its pristine landscape. This clash between preservation and development set the stage for one of the most important chapters in the history of the Grand Canyon: its designation as a protected national treasure.

The early 20th century saw a growing movement in the United States to conserve the country's natural resources and protect its most iconic landscapes from exploitation. One of the leading figures in this movement was President Theodore Roosevelt, who was an avid outdoorsman and a passionate advocate for conservation. In 1903, Roosevelt visited the Grand Canyon and was so struck by its beauty and grandeur that he made it a priority to ensure its preservation for future generations. In a speech given at the canyon's South Rim, he famously urged Americans to "leave it as it is," declaring that "man can only mar it." Roosevelt's commitment to conservation led to the Grand Canyon being designated a National Monument in 1908, under the authority of the Antiquities Act. This designation marked a significant step in the protection of the canyon, but it would take several more decades of advocacy before the Grand Canyon would achieve its full status as a National Park.

In 1919, after years of lobbying by conservationists and public figures, including John Muir and the National Park Service's first director, Stephen Mather, the Grand Canyon was officially designated as a National Park by an act of Congress. The establishment of Grand Canyon National Park was a major victory for the conservation movement and cemented the canyon's place as one of the most cherished natural landmarks in the United States. The park's creation also marked a turning point in the broader effort to protect America's natural heritage, setting a precedent for the establishment of other national parks and monuments across the country.

Throughout the 20th century, the Grand Canyon continued to play a central role in American history, both as a symbol of the country's natural beauty and as a site of scientific and cultural significance. During the 1930s, the construction of the Hoover Dam, located just downstream from the canyon, brought new attention to the Colorado River and its role in shaping the canyon. The dam, which was a marvel of engineering at the time, helped to control the flow of the river and provide water and electricity to the rapidly growing cities of the Southwest. However, it also had significant ecological impacts on the Grand Canyon, altering the river's natural flow and affecting the ecosystems that depended on it. The debate over the dam's construction highlighted the ongoing tension between development and conservation in the region, a theme that has persisted throughout the canyon's history.

In the decades that followed, the Grand Canyon became an increasingly popular destination for tourists from around the world, with millions of visitors flocking to the park each year to experience its awe-inspiring beauty. The development of infrastructure, including roads, lodges, and visitor centers, made the canyon more accessible to the public, while efforts to preserve its natural and cultural resources continued. In the 1960s and 1970s, the environmental movement gained momentum, and the Grand Canyon once again became a focal point for debates over land use and conservation. Proposals to build more dams along the Colorado River, as well as plans for large-scale mining and development projects, sparked widespread public outcry and led to the passage of laws aimed at protecting the canyon from further degradation.

Today, the Grand Canyon remains one of the most iconic symbols of the American wilderness and a testament to the country's commitment to preserving its natural wonders for future generations. Its place in American history is not only defined by its geological significance but also by the stories of the people who have lived in, explored, and fought to protect it. From the Native American tribes who first called the canyon home, to the explorers and scientists who charted its depths, to the conservationists who worked to ensure its preservation, the Grand Canyon's history is a rich and multifaceted one that continues to inspire and captivate people from all walks of life.

In the 21st century, the challenges of protecting the Grand Canyon remain as pressing as ever. Climate change, increasing tourism, and the ongoing demands for water and resources in the arid Southwest pose new threats to the canyon and its ecosystems. However, the legacy of conservation that began with figures like John Wesley Powell and Theodore Roosevelt continues to shape the way we view and manage the canyon today. The Grand Canyon is not just a place of natural beauty; it is a symbol of the enduring power of nature and the importance of preserving our planet's most precious resources for future generations. In this way, the Grand Canyon's place in American history is not just a story of the past, but an ongoing narrative of stewardship, responsibility, and awe-inspiring wonder.

Epilogue

You've made it to the end of *All About Grand Canyon: A Kid's Guide to Nature's Greatest Wonder*! Along the way, you've uncovered the secrets of one of the most amazing places on Earth. From its ancient rock layers to its diverse wildlife, the Grand Canyon is truly a place full of wonders. You've traveled back in time to learn how the canyon was carved over millions of years, met the Native American tribes who call it home, and even imagined the thrill of standing on the edge of the canyon's towering cliffs.

But just because this book is ending doesn't mean your adventure has to stop here. The Grand Canyon is always changing, and there's so much more to discover, whether you visit in person one day or continue learning from afar. Maybe you'll become a scientist who studies the canyon's geology, a park ranger who helps protect it, or a nature lover who explores its trails.

The Grand Canyon belongs to all of us, and it's up to us to take care of it for future generations. So, next time you hear about this mighty canyon, remember the incredible stories it holds and the importance of protecting such natural wonders.

As you close this book, think about the other great places around the world that are waiting for you to explore. Every adventure, whether big or small, starts with curiosity—just like the journey you've taken through the Grand Canyon. Keep exploring, keep asking questions, and keep discovering the wonders of the world!

The End.